1991

ZAGAT SAN FRANCISCO BAY AREA RESTAURANT SURVEY

Edited by Anthony Dias Blue
Coordinated by Jack Weiner

Published and Distributed by

ZAGAT SURVEY
4 Columbus Circle
New York, New York 10019
212-977-6000

ACKNOWLEDGMENTS

This book is based on the ratings and articulate comments of more than a thousand dedicated restaurant-goers in the Bay Area. We dedicate this book to them. It is truly theirs. Our special thanks to Lisa Bransten, who helped organize all the data which was checked by researchers Carol Seibert and Mike Sherman. We also thank Michael Bauer, Susan Dinsmore, Nick Freud, Paula Hamilton, Lisa Hoska, Leroy Meshel, Howard Nemerovski, Marjorie Rice, Ted Russel, Carolyn Snyder, Ira Zuckerman, the American Institute of Wine and Food and the San Francisco Fair National Wine Competition. Naturally, we must also express gratitude to the chefs and restaurant owners who work so diligently to make the Bay Area one of the most exciting culinary centers in the world.

FOR INFORMATION
ON ORDERING

ZAGAT UNITED STATES TRAVEL SURVEY
3 volumes covering over 1400 hotels, resorts,
spas, airlines and car rental companies

or

ZAGAT RESTAURANT SURVEYS
Arizona; Atlanta; Baltimore; Boston; Chicago;
Dallas–Fort Worth; Houston; Kansas City;
London; Los Angeles–Orange County–
San Diego; Montreal; New Orleans;
New York City; Suburban New York City;
Pacific Northwest; Philadelphia; St. Louis;
San Francisco and Washington, D.C.

or

ZAGAT NYC MARKETPLACE SURVEY
covering food, wine and entertaining sources

Call 212-977-6000
or write to:

Zagat Survey
4 Columbus Circle
New York, New York 10019

CONTENTS

INTRODUCTION

Here are the results of our 1991 *San Francisco Bay Area Restaurant Survey* covering 540 restaurants in the Bay Area. Over 1,000 people participated in this *Survey*. Since the participants dined out on an average of 3.5 times per week, this Survey is based on more than 180,000 meals eaten in area restaurants during the past year.

Knowing that the quality of this *Survey* is the direct result of their thoughtful voting and commentary, we sincerely thank each of this year's participants. They include numerous professionals, business executives, members of local food and wine societies and just plain folks – food lovers all.

We are especially grateful to Anthony Dias Blue, the nationally syndicated food and wine radio and television commentator and columnist, and his assistant, Jack Weiner. They devoted much of the past year to helping organize the *Survey* and to editing the results.

By regularly surveying large numbers of local restaurant-goers, we think we have achieved a uniquely current and reliable guide. We hope you agree. On the assumption that most people want a "quick fix" on the places at which they are considering eating, we have tried to be concise and to provide handy indexes.

We invite you to be a reviewer in our next Survey. To do so, simply send a stamped, self-addressed, business-size envelope to ZAGAT SURVEY, 4 Columbus Circle, New York, N.Y. 10019 so that we will be able to contact you. Each participant will receive a free copy of the next *San Francisco Bay Area Restaurant Survey* when it is published.

Your comments, suggestions and criticisms of this year's *Survey* are also solicited. There is always room for improvement – with your help.

New York, New York   Nina and Tim Zagat
December 15, 1990

FOREWORD

San Franciscans must eat out more than the denizens of any other American city. More than 50 cents of every Bay Area dollar spent on food is spent in restaurants. Add to that the steady stream of visitors to the sparkling city by the bay, and you can figure why a relatively small city (only the fourth largest in California) is consistently voted one of the best restaurant towns in the United States.

Food and wine are the main topic at Bay Area soirees and down on Montgomery Street. While New Yorkers are discussing the latest Wall Street takeover bid and Chicagoans are waxing poetic over pork bellies, San Franciscans will be sharing notes on the newest Hakka restaurant out in the Avenues or the new trendy glitterati hangout in SOMA. Bay Area people take their restaurants seriously which is why over 1,000 of them dutifully filled out their lengthy Zagat questionnaires, loading them with kudos and brickbats and plenty of wit.

Bay Area restaurants continue to offer the best variety of Asian ("Oriental" is no longer an acceptable word) cuisines in the country. But don't overlook the dazzling array of French, Italian and, of course, California restaurants in virtually every neighborhood of this sophisticated city.

It should also be noted that it is now a law in California that all restaurants have wheelchair access and non-smoking sections.

The *1991 Zagat* is an all-new version, with every restaurant review newly-written and based on comments made by our reviewers. Once again it is a mirror that shows the lively, dynamic Northern California restaurant scene in all its glory.

San Francisco, CA   Anthony Dias Blue
December 15, 1990

EXPLANATION OF RATINGS AND SYMBOLS

FOOD, DECOR and **SERVICE** are each rated on a scale of 0 to 30 in columns marked **F, D** and **S:**

> 0-9 = poor to fair
> 10-19 = good to very good
> 20-25 = very good to excellent
> 26-30 = extraordinary to perfection

The **COST** column, headed by a **C,** reflects the estimated price of a dinner with one drink and tip. As a rule of thumb, lunch will cost 25 percent less.

An **Asterisk (*)** after a restaurant's name means the number of persons who voted on the restaurant is too low to be statistically reliable; **L** for late means the restaurant serves after 11 PM; **S** and **M** means it is open on Sunday and Monday, respectively; and **X** means no credit cards are accepted.

By way of **Commentary**, we attempt to summarize the comments of the *Survey* participants, occasionally retaining a prior year's comments where appropriate. The prefix **U** means comments were uniform; **M** means they were mixed.

The names of the restaurants with the highest overall ratings and greatest popularity are printed in solid capital letters, e.g., **"POSTRIO."**

If we do not show ratings on a restaurant, it is either an important **newcomer** or a popular **write-in;** however, comments are included and the estimated cost, including one drink and tip, is indicated by the following symbols:

> **I** = below $15
> **M** = $15 to $30
> **E** = $30 to $50
> **VE** = $50 or above

9

BAY AREA'S MOST POPULAR RESTAURANTS*

Each of our one thousand reviewers has been asked to name his or her five favorite restaurants. The 40 spots most frequently named, in order of their popularity, are:

1.	Postrio	21.	Auberge du Soleil/N
2.	Masa's	22.	China Moon Cafe
3.	Stars	23.	Kuleto's
4.	Fleur de Lys	24.	Bay Wolf
5.	Square One	25.	Acqurello
6.	The Lark Creek Inn	26.	Buca Giovani
7.	Chez Panisse	27.	Sedona Grill & Bar
8.	Zuni Cafe	28.	231 Ellsworth
9.	Cafe at Chez Panisse	29.	Fresh Cream/S
10.	Tra Vigne/N	30.	Lalime's
11.	Campton Place	31.	Roti
12.	Il Fornaio/S	32.	Bix
13.	Domaine Chandon/N	33.	Fog City Diner
14.	Green's	34.	Tommy Toy's Chinois
15.	Donatello	35.	Janot's
16.	L'Avenue	36.	Cafe Beaujolais/N
17.	Hayes Street Grill	37.	Ristorante Milano
18.	The Blue Fox	38.	Le Castel
19.	Mustard's Grill/N	39.	Rodin
20.	La Folie	40.	Olivetto

Most of the restaurants on the above list are among the area's more expensive, but Californians are also bargain hunters. Accordingly, we have listed roughly 140 "Best Buys" on pages 16 and 17. This Survey demonstrates that people, more than ever, are looking for value-oriented restaurants. Fortunately, the San Francisco area has an abundance of wonderful simple American and ethnic places that fill the bill.

---

* All restaurants are in the San Francisco metropolitan area unless otherwise noted. "S" indicates South of San Francisco and "N" indicates North of San Francisco.

TOP RATINGS*

TOP 40 FOOD RATINGS
(In order of rating)

28 – Masa's
27 – Fleur de Lys
 Fresh Cream/S
 Chez Panisse
26 – Terra/N
 Postrio
 Domaine Chandon
 Lark Creek Inn, The
 La Folie
 Trilogy/N
 Emile's/S
 Thep Phanom
25 – Le Castel
 Campton Place
 Cafe at Chez Panisse
 Stars
 L'Avenue
 House of Nanking
 John Ash & Co./N
 Chez T.J./S

French Laundry/N
Amelio's
Rodin
French Room, The
Cafe Beaujolais/N
Le Mouton Noir/S
Helmand
24 – Square One
 Mustard's Grill/N
 Chateau Souvrain/N
 Ristorante Milano
 Donatello
 Kabuto Sushi
 Kenwood Restaurant
 Green's
 Le Papillon
 Vivande Porta Via
 231 Ellsworth
 Sedona Grill & Bar
 Nan Yang

TOP SPOTS BY CUISINE

Top American
26 – Lark Creek Inn, The
25 – John Ash & Co./N
 Campton Place
 Cafe Beaujolais/N
24 – Kenwood Restaurant

Top Californian
28 – Campbell House
27 – Chez Panisse
26 – Postrio
 Trilogy/N
25 – Stars

Top Chinese
25 – House of Nanking
23 – Yank Sing
 Tommy Toy's Chinoise
 North Sea Village
 Tung Fong

Top Continental
25 – French Room, The
23 – Pavillion Room
22 – Mirabelle
 Fournou's Oven
 Dal Baffo

---

* Excluding restaurants with voting too low to be statistically reliable.

11

Top Deli

18 – Brother's
17 – Saul's
16 – Max's Opera Cafe
14 – Acropolis Deli
— Vivande Porta Via

Top French Bistro

23 – Le St. Tropez
Brasserie Tomo
22 – Le Trou
21 – Le Piano Zinc
20 – South Park Cafe

Top French Classic

28 – Masa's
27 – Fleur de Lys
26 – La Folie
Emile's
25 – Le Castel

Top French Nouvelle

26 – Domaine Chandon
25 – Rodin
Amelio's
Le Mouton Noir
23 – Starmont

Top Hotel Dining

28 – Masa's
26 – Postrio
25 – French Room, The
Campton Place
24 – Donatello

Top Indian

23 – Indian Oven
21 – North India Rest.
20 – India House
18 – Gaylord
— Sue's Kitchen

Top Italian Northern

26 – Terra/N
Giuliano's
24 – Ristorante Milano
Donatello
23 – Tra Vigne/N

Top Italian Traditional

24 – Vivande Porta Via
Piatti/N
23 – Acquerello
Paolo's/S
Parma

Top Japanese

25 – Tanuki
24 – Kabuto Sushi
23 – Ebisu
22 – Yoshida-Ya
20 – Osome

Top Mexican

23 – La Taqueria
Casa Aguila
22 – Mom Is Cooking
20 – Corona Bar & Grill
Taqueria Mission

Top Offbeat/Sleeper

26 – Thep Phanom
25 – Cafe at Chez Panisse
21 – Seoul Garden
Plearn Thai Cuisine
19 – Geva's

Top Oyster Bars

24 – Swan Oyster Bar
20 – La Rocca's Oyster Bar
19 – Pacific Heights Bar
Gulf Coast Oyster Bar
18 – Bentley's

Top Pizza

22 – Vicolo Pizzeria
Tommaso's
21 – Il Fornaio/S
19 – Milano Pizzeria
18 – Spuntino

Top Rated Newcomers

26 – Chantilly Francais/S
24 – Nan Yan
23 – Park Grill
22 – Pacific Grill
Enoteca Mastro/S

Top Seafood

24 – Swan Oyster Depot
21 – Sam's Grill Seafood
     Tadich Grill
     Squire Restaurant
16 – Pacific Fresh/S

Top Southeast Asian

24 – Nan Yang
23 – Angkor Palace
     Cambodia House
     Mandalay
     Phnom Penh

Top Steakhouses

22 – House of Prime Rib
     Harris' Restaurant
21 – Alfred's
19 – Izzy's Steak/Chop
18 – Original Joe's

Top Unrated Newcomers

— Brava Terrace
— Caribbean Zone
— Laghi
— Monsoon
— Palio d'Asti

Top Vegetarian

24 – Green's
19 – Vegi Food
17 – Diamond Street
16 – Milly's
14 – Long Life Vegi House

Top Worth A Trip

26 – Terra/N
     Domaine Chandon/N
     Lark Creek Inn; The
25 – John Ash & Co./N
     Chez T.J./S

TOP 40 OVERALL DECOR
(In order of rating)

28 – Act IV

27 – Auberge Du Soleil/N
French Room, The
Postrio
Domaine Chandon/N

26 – Etrusca
Tommy Toy's Chinoise
Fleur de Lys
Victor's
Starmont/N
Tra Vigne/N
Campton Place

25 – Chateau Souvrain/N
Masa's
Carnelian Room
Lark Creek Inn, The
French Laundry/N
John Ash & Co./N
Silks

24 – El Paseo

Bix
Casa Madrona
Lascaux
Park Grill
1001 Nob Hill
Donatello
Tourelle
Ernie's
Madrona Manor/N
Squire Restaurant

23 – Cafe Majestic
Fournou's Oven
Mandarin, The
Pierre at Meridien
Pacific Grill
Caprice, The
Il Fornaio/S
Terra/N
Le Mouton Noir/S
Big Four

TOP VIEWS AND VISTAS
(In alphabetical order)

Alta Mira
Butler's
Caprice, The
Carnelian Room
Casa Madrona
Cliff House
Domaine Chandon/N
Gaylord
Green's
Guaymas

Harbor Village
Horizons
Julius' Castle
Mandarin, The
Pavilion Room
Sam's Anchor Cafe
Starmont/N
Victor's
Waterfront

TOP ROOMS
(In alphabetical order)

Auberge du Soleil/N
Big Four
Blue Fox, The
Campton Place
Donatello
Ernie's
Fleur de Lys
Fournou's Ovens
French Laundry/N
French Room, The

Harris' Restaurant
Madrona Manor/N
Masa's
Pierre at Meridien
Postrio
Squire Restaurant, The
Starmont/N
Stars
Trader Vic's

TOP 40 OVERALL SERVICE
(In order of rating)

27 – Masa's

25 – Emile's/S
Fleur De Lys
Le Castel
Fresh Cream/S
Campton Place

24 – Amelio's
French Laundry/N
French Room, The
Le Mouton Noir/S
Domaine Chandon/N
Le Club
La Folie
Donatello

23 – Acquerello
Chez Panisse
Ernie's
Tommy Toy's Chinoise
Pierre at Meridien
Blue Fox, The

Fournou's Ovens
John Ash & Co./N
Lark Creek Inn, The
Plumed Horse, The/S
Parma
Terra/N
L'Escargot
Auberge Du Soleil/N
Victor's
Squire Restaurant
Rodin
231 Ellsworth
Dal Baffo

22 – Helmand
L'Avenue
Barbarossa/S
El Paseo
Zola's
Pacific Grill
Postrio

BEST BUYS

SUPER BUYS*
(Possible to stuff yourself for $12 or less)

Ace Cafe
American Chow
Angkor Palace
Angkor Wat
Betty's Ocean View Diner
Bill's Place
Bohemian Cigar Store
Brandy Ho's on Broadway
Brazen Head
Brother's Delicatessen
Cactus Cafe
Cafe Claude
Cafe Fanny
Cafe For All Seasons
Caffe Roma
Cambodia House
Casa Aguila
Cheer's Cafe
Dipsea Cafe
Doidge's Kitchen
Don Ramon's Mexican
Doug's BBQ
Ebisu
Emerald Garden
Ernesto's
Fat Apple's
Fountain Court
Fung Lum
Hamburger Mary's
Helmand
Hong Kong Tea House
House of Nanking
Indian Oven
Island Cafe
Isobune Sushi
Jade Villa

Juan's Place
Khan Toke Thai House
Kirin
La Mediterranee
La Taqueria
Little Henry's
Mama's Royal Cafe
Manora's Thai Cuisine
Max's Diner
Mel's Diner
Mom Is Cooking
Nan Yang
Ocean Restaurant
Ocean City
Phnom Penh
Roosevelt Tamale Parlor
Royal Thai
Sally's
San Francisco BBQ
Sanppo
Sears Fine Food
Siam Cuisine
Spuntino
Swan Oyster Depot
Taiwan Restaurant
Taqueria Mission
Thep Phanom
Tommaso's
Tommy's Joynt
Ton Kiang
Trio Cafe
Triple Rock Brewery
Tung Fong
Vicolo Pizzeria
Vivande Porta Via
Yank Sing

---

* Most Indian and many Chinese places offer unlimited,
inexpensive buffet lunches..

GOOD VALUES

(A bit more expensive, but worth every penny)

Abalonetti*
Australian Rest./S
Aux Delices
Balboa Cafe
Barrio Fiesta
Basta Pasta
Cadillac Bar & Restaurant
Cafe At Chez Panisse*
Cafe de Bordeaux
Cafe Riggio
Caffe Venezia
Capp's Corner
Carrera's
Chef Chu's
Chevys
China Pavilion
City Block
Clark's by the Bay/S
Cliff House
Curbside Cafe
DePaula's Rest. & Pizzeria
Diamond St. Restaurant*
Downtown Bakery/N
Eddie Rickenbacher's
Emerald Garden
Feng Nian
Flower Lounge
Gertie's Chesapeake Cafe
Golden Turtle
Gray Whale/N
Guaymas
Gulf Coast Oyster Bar
Himalaya Rest.
La Mexicana
Little City Antipasti Bar

Little Henry's
Little Italy
Little Joe's
London Wine Bar, The
Long Life Vegi House
Lori's Diner
Mandalay
Mifune
Milano Joe's
Milly's
Mom Is Cooking
Narai
Pacific Heights Bar & Grill
Perry's
Phnom Penh
Plearn Thai Cuisine
Ramona's
Saul's Delicatessen
Sam's Grill & Seafood
Scott's Seafood Grill*/S
South Park Cafe
Squid's Cafe
Stars Cafe
Station House Cafe/N
Straits Cafe
Taco Al Pastor/S
Ton Kiang
Tortola Restaurant
Trattoria Contadina
Trio Cafe
U.S. Restaurant
Washington Sq. Bar & Grill
Ya Ya's
Yuen Yung
Yuet Lee

---

* Prix fixe menus that are good values.

ALPHABETICAL
DIRECTORY
OF RESTAURANTS

San Francisco

Ace Cafe/LSM | 15 | 15 | 12 | $14 |
1539 Folsom St. (11th St.), 621-4752
*U – "You'll feel more at home in black trappings" at this
"funky" new SOMA hangout, a "great late-night spot"
that caters to the "hip and trendy"; the "imaginative,
but not very consistent" Californian menu at this casual
haunt wins kudos for it's usually "excellent" sandwiches,
desserts and drinks; "great industrial decor", a "fun
staff" and low prices keep this ace hopping.*

Acquerello | 23 | 21 | 23 | $39 |
1722 Sacramento St. (Van Ness Ave.), 567-5432
*U – A "strong newcomer", this "intimate" Van
Ness/Polk spot is "everything an upscale Italian
restaurant should be", no surprise given the talented
team of ex-Donatello's; "superb" food (especially
"stellar desserts"), "fine Italian wines" and "quietly
attentive" service (from Giancarlo and his staff) make it
"one of the very best Italian choices in SF"; some find
the decor "sophisticated", others label it "spartan."*

Acropolis Deli*/SM | 14 | 5 | 12 | $10 |
5217 Geary Blvd. (16th Ave.), 751-9661
*U – Only in SF would you find the wacky ethnic mix
this Chinese-owned, Greek-named Russian deli
provides in Richmond; besides being unusual, it's also
pretty good, with "yummy cottage cheese pancakes",
"wonderful sandwiches" and "the best [homemade]
sour cream in SF"; service can be "rough and crabby",
but it's a deli, after all.*

Act IV/LSM | 16 | 28 | 20 | $35 |
Inn at the Opera, 333 Fulton Ave. (Franklin St.), 863-8400
*M – This "very intimate and romantic" Civic Center
French gets unanimous raves for its "cushy" and
"elegant" decor and convenience to the Performing
Arts Center; its "spotty" classical cuisine "doesn't
measure up", prompting some to call it "just a very
pretty face" and "wretchedly overpriced"; still, it's
"great for brunch" or a "pre-opera seduction."*

Adriana's/SM | 21 | 14 | 18 | $24 |

999 Andersen Dr. (Bell St.), San Rafael, 454-8000

M – This unpretentious Marin Italian is a neighborhood favorite for "great fresh pasta" and "excellent seafood" at reasonable prices; fans say "Mama patrols the kitchen and the results show", though a few dissenters find the fare "uninspired"; likewise, some find the setting "upbeat and bright", others call it "stark" and "coffee shop" like.

Adriatic/S | 16 | 15 | 15 | $21 |

1755 Polk St. (Washington St.), 771-4035

U – A "nice neighborhood fish restaurant" in the Van Ness-Polk area that "always satisfies" with "good fresh" seafood at moderate prices, "attentive service" and an "unpretentious" atmosphere add to its appeal; particularly busy at lunchtime.

A la Carte/SM | 20 | 16 | 19 | $25 |

1453 Dwight Way (Sacramento St.), Berkeley, 548-2322

M – Fans call this "small and cozy" East Bay neighborhood haunt "a French gem", with "imaginative" and mostly good food served in a romantic ambiance; foes dismiss it as "tasteless" and overpriced.

Alejandro's Sociedad/LSM | 17 | 15 | 15 | $22 |

1840 Clement St. (19th Ave.), 668-1184

M – "Good paella", "quick and friendly" service and a "festive Latin atmosphere" are the main draws at this loud Richmond Spanish-Peruvian-Mexican; tapas are tasty, but the rest of the menu draws mixed reviews and some say overall quality "has slipped in recent years"; a "decent value for the money" and "great fun" despite "long waits even with reservations."

Alessia/S | 15 | 15 | 15 | $22 |

23 Ross Common (Redwood St.), Ross, 925-9619

M – This "unreliable" Italian is "imaginative" and "good" vs. "adequate" and "not exciting"; dining on the lovely outdoor patio at this "very Marin" spot is "fabulous on a warm night", and the "attractive" romantic interior is perfect for "quiet luncheons and dinners" – it's almost enough to make you forget about the "small portions at high prices."

Alfred's/SM | 21 | 16 | 20 | $31 |
886 Broadway (Powell St.), 781-7058
U – "Even the dust hasn't changed since the 1950s" at this "classic old-time" North Beach steakhouse; fans rave, the corn-fed beef is "the best steak in the Bay area", others complain about the rest of the Italian menu; true to type, it has a "dark heavy", "bordello-like" setting and the waiters, some of whom appear to have been "born in the restaurant", are "characters out of a Damon Runyon novel."

Alioto's Restaurant | 15 | 15 | 15 | $25 |
8 Fisherman's Wharf (Jefferson St.), 673-0183
M – Many dismiss this large Fisherman's Wharf seafood joint as an overpriced "tourist trap", others claim it serves "pretty decent" fish and praise the recently added traditional Sicilian dishes; a "relaxed atmosphere" and "pleasant view" are pluses.

Alta Mira Restaurant and Hotel/SM | 11 | 22 | 14 | $26 |
Alta Mira Hotel, 125 Bulkley Ave. (Princess St.), Sausalito, 332-1350
U – "Ignore the food" and concentrate on the "view" (sometimes clouded by long waits and perfunctory service) and "great al fresco dining" on the deck of this Sausalito tourist attraction; "take friends from Cleveland to brunch on a sunny day" and they'll be so dazzled they'll never notice the "world's worst seafood salad" and other culinary backfires.

AMELIO'S/SM | 25 | 21 | 24 | $46 |
1630 Powell St. (bet. Green & Union Sts.), 397-4339
U – This "very romantic" North Beach French received a much-needed shot in the arm when chef Jacky Robert (formerly of Ernie's) joined the crew; his Nouvelle cuisine is "precious", "exciting" and "wonderfully creative"; the food, fine wine list and "old SF atmosphere" make it a "very pleasurable experience" (in spite of the dark decor that "needs a facelift"); expensive but unique.

American Chow/SM | 16 | 11 | 15 | $14 |
340 Division St. (bet. 10th & Bryant Sts.), 863-1212
U – "Funky" SOMA diner underneath the freeway that serves up "good, sensible, trustworthy" food (soups, burgers, homemade pies, etc.), plus a surprisingly good wine list; "kooky waitresses" and a "delightfully unpretentious" ambiance make it "great fun."

Angkor Palace/SM | 23 | 20 | 20 | $19 |

1769 Lombard St. (Octavia St.), 931-2830

U – Attractive Marina Cambodian that offers "a transcultural experience"; the "unique" and "wonderful" food features "flavors so clean they sparkle" – don't miss the "beautiful salads" and the Cambodian crepe; service is smooth and low-key, the atmosphere "quiet and relaxing" and prices modest.

Angkor Wat/S | 22 | 17 | 20 | $20 |

4217 Geary Blvd. (6th Ave.), 221-7887

U – Very popular Richmond Cambodian that offers "complex flavors" and "attentive service" in a "beautiful setting"; the food is exotic and often "exquisite" and the "wonderful" floor show of temple dancers is an added attraction; dinner only.

A. Sabella's/SM | 12 | 14 | 15 | $25 |

2766 Taylor St. (Fisherman's Wharf), 771-6775

M – "Decent for the wharf", this veteran "tourist spot" has been packing them in for over 60 years with its "nice view" and mass-produced Italian seafood served by an efficient, old-time staff; critics yawn "ho-hum."

Asta | – | – | – | M |

101 Spear St. (Mission St.), 495-2782

Named after the dog from the popular Thin Man movies, this new Eclectic restaurant in the renovated Downtown Rincon Center is big on portions but falls short on service; decor feels like the '40s, but prices are definitely the '90s.

Augusta's/S | 17 | 15 | 16 | $23 |

2955 Telegraph Ave. (Ashby Ave.), Berkeley, 548-3140

M – A "lovely" outdoor garden and "friendly" feel are the main assets of this Berkeley seafood spot; the food is "uninspired" and service operates in "slo-mo", but it's not a bad choice for leisurely outdoor lunches; for best results, "stick with simple dishes."

Aux Delices/SM | 16 | 10 | 15 | $16 |

1002 Potrero Ave. (22nd St.), 285-3196

2327 Polk St. (Green St.), 928-4977

U – Modest Potrero Hill and Polk Street spots offering good Vietnamese cuisine in comfortable digs; "lunch is the best deal", but at these prices, it's all a bargain.

Avenue Grill/S
| 20 | 17 | 19 | $25 |

44 E. Blithedale Ave. (Sunnyside Ave.), Mill Valley, 388-6003

U – "Funky" California-style roadhouse that serves up huge portions of spicy meatloaf, chicken, garlic mashed potatoes and other "hearty American comfort food with a sense of humor"; "noisy and jammed", it's a "hot Mill Valley hangout" that's "great for people-watching"; "if depressed, go here to cheer up."

Baci/SM
| 18 | 17 | 15 | $24 |

247 Shoreline Hwy. (Tam Junction), Mill Valley, 381-2022

M – Fans say this stylish Marin County yuppie scene is a "pleasant place" with "delicious pasta" and pizza and other "good Italian food", but critics aren't blowing any kisses – they complain of "average" food, noise and the "world's worst service."

Bahia
| 16 | 16 | 16 | $21 |

41 Franklin St. (Market St.), 626-3306

M – For "fun and different" dining try this Brazilian; its "wonderful garlicky shrimp and stews" and other "hearty" dishes will fill you up, and the "festive environment and music" and "diverse crowd" will keep you entertained, all for a moderate price; critics say the food is "just ok" and service is "so slow."

Balboa Cafe/S
| 18 | 16 | 16 | $21 |

3199 Fillmore St. (Greenwich St.), 921-3944

U – "A great place to see SF at play", this Fillmore Street meet-market will provide you with the "best burger in town" and , if you're lucky, a date for the evening; while best known for its yuppie singles action, it has "surprisingly good" food, too.

Bardelli's/SM
| 15 | 18 | 18 | $25 |

243 O'Farrell St. (Mason St.), 982-0243

U – "One of the last of the old-fashioned places", this Downtown Italian draws an older local crowd thanks to its "time warp nostalgia", "great stained glass decor" and unexciting but "totally reliable" food; it's a little "tired but pleasant", with a "quiet, leisurely feeling" and service that's good if "a little perfunctory."

Barrio Fiesta/SMX
| 18 | 20 | 20 | $18 |

909 Antoinette Lane (Chestnut St.), 871-8703

U – This modest South City Filipino eatery offers an auspicious introduction to an obscure cuisine – expect "unusual combinations of flavors"; try the kare kare and the special shrimp, and come back again.

Basta Pasta/LSM | 13 | 13 | 14 | $20 |
1268 Grant Ave. (Vallejo St.), 434-2248
*M – Fans say this raffish "lively" North Beach Italian
serves good pasta, fish and other "basic decent food"
in a kitschy Victorian setting; critics blast its "formica
decor with pasta to match", calling it "barely passable"
and "getting worse every year"; low prices and late
hours are undisputed assets.*

Bayon, The/S | 19 | 14 | 20 | $21 |
2018 Lombard St. (Webster St.), 922-1400
*M – "Elegant" Marina Cambodian that blends Asian
and French culinary ideas with intriguing results; the
food is "beautifully prepared" and "delicious", as well
as "an exceptional value"; some say the decor is "too
austere" and service too "slow", but all in all this is
"one of the best deals in town."*

BAY WOLF/SM | 23 | 19 | 22 | $31 |
3853 Piedmont Ave. (40th St.), Oakland, 655-6004
*U – This 1970s "California cuisine classic" has made
the transition to the 1990s with grace; the changing
menu sometimes verges on the "bizarre", but "hits
much more often than it misses" and is enhanced by
an excellent and fairly priced wine list; service is
"friendly", decor "intimate" and "comfortable", and
"lunch on the terrace is delightful."*

Beethoven/SM | 19 | 18 | 20 | $25 |
1701 Powell St. (Union St.), 391-4488
*U – "One of the best German restaurants this side of
Chicago", this "cozy and comfortable" North Beach
place offers a "warm atmosphere" and a full menu of
"hearty, teutonic eats"; yes, Hans, the food is "heavy",
but it's "wholesome" and "dependable" and the
"romantic" ambiance and gemutlich service (not to
mention the beer) make it taste even better.*

Bella Vista/S | 20 | 22 | 19 | $34 |
13451 Skyline Blvd. (5 miles south of I-92), Woodside,
851-1229
*U – The ambiance and view take top honors at this
pricey, romantic Peninsula Continental; the food can be
"old-style and heavy" but service is friendly and the
clientele can be outrageously eclectic (everyone from
"bikers to yuppies and professors"); there's no rushing
here – "it's an all-evening experience"; bring your
significant other.*

Bella Voce/LSM $\qquad$ | 17 | 23 | 22 | $31 |
Fairmont Hotel, 950 Mason St. (California St.), 772-5199
*U – If you like Puccini with your pizza, you'll love this
Nob Hill hotel dining room, where the costumed staff
belts out opera as they serve "decent" Italian food;
though the "singers are better than the food", a
majority calls it a "most enjoyable" experience.*

Benihana/LS $\qquad$ | 14 | 15 | 18 | $23 |
1737 Post St. (Webster St.), 563-4844
2074 Valco Fashion Park (Rte. 280, Wolfe Rd.),
Cupertino, 408-253-1221
*M – "Not for serious diners", this "gimmicky"
Japanese chain features grilled meats and veggies
cooked tableside by flashy, knife-wielding showman
chefs; fans call it "entertaining" and "fun", a "great
place to take kids"; critics call it "an expensive joke."*

Bentley's $\qquad$ | 18 | 18 | 17 | $26 |
185 Sutter St. (Kearny St.), 989-6895
*M – "Great oysters" – raw, pan-fried, in chowders – are
the top attraction at this Downtown seafood emporium/
power lunch spot; the rest of the menu is "fresh" and
"well-prepared", but the rule is "the simpler the better
here"; upstairs is recommended for quieter dining away
from the noisy bar area – though the staff "sometimes
forgets you" up there.*

Betty's Ocean View Diner/X $\qquad$ | 21 | 16 | 16 | $14 |
1807 Fourth St. (Hearst Ave.), Berkeley, 644-3230
*U – "A great Berkeley scene", this "funky", "upbeat"
'50s-style diner is a local tradition for "marvelous
breakfasts" and other solid "good eats"; it has no
ocean view, but does have "friendly service", "the best
jukebox", long lines and a "very Berkeley" clientele.*

Big Four/SM $\qquad$ | 17 | 23 | 20 | $35 |
Huntington Hotel, 1075 California St. (Taylor St.),
771-1140
*M – The "four" were the industrial titans who ran SF in
the late 1800s; this pricey Nob Hill spot named after
them has "historically intriguing", "elegant men's club"
atmosphere and traditional food that's "nothing special"
but "consistent"; "great for breakfast meetings" and
power pow-wows.*

Bill's Place/SX | 13 | 8 | 12 | $12 |

2315 Clement St. (24th Ave.), 221-5262
*M – Richmond District burger place that's seen better
days; surveyors beef about "greasy", "tasteless"
burgers that are "a half step above McDonald's";
though the interior is "shabby", the "garden is nice on
a warm afternoon."*

BIX/SM | 20 | 24 | 20 | $31 |

56 Gold St. (bet. Jackson & Pacific Sts.), 433-6300
*U – This "sophisticated" and "very sexy" Downtown
supper club offers the "best martinis" in town and
remarkably good California contemporary cuisine
(don't miss the corn custard or chicken hash) created by
Fog City's Cindy Pawlcyn; have a cocktail and "enjoy
dining again" in a '40s-ish "neo-deco" setting that's
"right out of Nick and Nora Charles"; a chic bar scene
and great live music at dinner make this one of SF's
most happening spots.*

BLUE FOX, THE/SM | 23 | 23 | 23 | $49 |

659 Merchant St. (Montgomery St.), 981-1177
*U – "A true renaissance", this classic Downtown Italian
is earning high praise after its recent total renovation –
"bravo", "what a comeback", "better than ever";
"fabulous food", an excellent wine list and "almost too
much" service make it "one of the best"; some find the
elegant mirrors-and-colored setting "staid" and "stuffy."*

Blue Light Cafe, The/SM | 14 | 16 | 14 | $21 |

1979 Union St. (Buchanan St.), 922-5510
*U – There's "always a good-looking crowd" at this
trendy Union Street bar/restaurant owned by rock star
Boz Scaggs; the food (Buffalo chicken wings, chicken-
fried steak and the like) is "decent and reasonably
priced", but that's not why people come here; the real
draws are the bar scene, recorded music that's the
"best in SF" and "good people-watching.*

Bohemian Cigar Store | 19 | 15 | 14 | $11 |

566 Columbus Ave. (Union St.), 362-0536
*U – "A SF classic", this small, atmospheric North Beach
coffee house is a favorite local "hideout" thanks to
"the best cappuccino outside of Italy" and "foccacia
sandwiches that will send you to heaven and back";
"always crowded", it's "honest, genuine and lots of
fun", and though service can be slow, who cares? – it's
a "great place to people-watch" or "be alone on a cold,
foggy day."*

Bonta | 21 | 16 | 20 | $27 |
2223 Union St. (bet. Fillmore & Steiner Sts.), 929-0407
U – Tiny, intimate Union Street Northern Italian that
some call "the find of the year"; the food is "first-class" –
don't miss the "fine pastas", "risotto of my dreams" and
"the best tiramisu in town"; yes, it's crowded and noisy,
but "we love it anyway."

Brandy Ho's on Broadway | 19 | 12 | 15 | $15 |
450 Broadway (Kearny St.), 362-6268
U – "Hot or hotter" are the two mouth-tingling choices
at this "very spicy" North Beach version of Brandy
Ho's Chinatown original; most praise the "four-alarm
dishes" and "great smoked foods", but advise "bring
a handkerchief – you will sweat"; service is
"unpredictable" and some reviewers find the "fantasy
decor" "kind of eerie."

Brasserie Tomo* | 23 | 14 | 19 | $56 |
745 Columbus Ave. (Filbert St.), 296-7668
U – "Very expensive" North Beach French with
Japanese overtones; the food is "exquisite" and "very
creative" and the setting is "like being in France",
though "fawning" service can mar an otherwise lovely
meal; often empty, but "more should know about it."

Brazen Head/LSX | 17 | 18 | 18 | $20 |
3166 Buchanan St. (Greenwich St.), 921-7600
U – "Cheers West"; this "small and intimate"
neighborhood bar is a favorite local hangout thanks to
"large portions" of basic American fare (chops, burgers,
etc.), late hours, a "dark and cozy" setting and friendly
service; "get a regular to take you" for the best experience.

Bricks | 18 | 14 | 17 | $17 |
500 Brannan St. (4th St.), 543-2222
298 Pacific St. (Battery St.), 788-2222
M – "Nothing special", this SOMA cafe is just a "good
burgers and beer" place with a "clean, bright" and
"comfy" setting that can get "awfully smoky and loud";
while some call it "a zero", others call it a "favorite"
and good for takeout, too.

Brother's Delicatessen/S | 18 | 8 | 14 | $13 |
1351 Howard Ave. (El Camino), Burlingame, 343-2311
M – "The only game in town, but a great deli it ain't";
still, this Chinese-owned Jewish deli has fans for its
"wonderful" cabbage soup, potato pancakes and
"chicken liver to die for", as well as its "back to New
Jersey atmosphere"; those who've tasted the real thing,
however, grouse, "if this is the best in the Bay Area,
we'll make our own matzoh balls."

F	D	S	C

Bruno's/LS

| 14 | 11 | 16 | $18 |

2389 Mission St. (20th St.), 641-1144

U – "Pleasant enough for an old-fashioned Italian", this neighborhood hangout offers "lots of food for the money", even if it isn't much more than adequate; antique waiters with personality to spare are one of the main attractions.

Buca Giovani

| 21 | 17 | 18 | $27 |

800 Greenwich St. (Mason St.), 776-7766

U – A "nice blend of down-to-earth and sophisticated", this popular North Beach Italian serves "earthy and authentic" Tuscan food in a "cavelike" basement setting; most praise the "excellent fresh pasta" and "great veal", though a few say the food can be "hit or miss"; some find the setting "cozy" and "romantic", others find it "dark", "musty" and often "noisy and hectic"; overall, though, it's "one of the best old-world Italians" in the area.

Bucci's/MX

| – | – | – | M |

6121 Hollis St. (Powell St.), Emeryville, 547-4725

Northern Italian served in a converted brick warehouse in the East Bay with good pizza and calzone, pasta and daily specials; patio dining is especially pleasant at lunch; moderately priced but no plastic.

Butler's/S

| 20 | 21 | 19 | $31 |

625 Redwood Hwy. (Seminary Dr.), Mill Valley, 383-1900

U – A "classic Californian" in both taste and look, this "Marin mainstay" serves "wonderfully inventive" and "reliably good" food in a stylish and relaxed setting, complete with a "fantastic view of Mt. Tam at sunset"; "friendly" service adds to a "very pleasant" experience.

Cactus Cafe/X

| 19 | 11 | 15 | $12 |

393 Miller Ave. (La Goma St.), Mill Valley, 388-8226

U – "Cheap and casual" Marin Mexican that specializes in "fabulous burritos, tacos, tortas", etc., with a variety of "innovative" fillings (how about a "tongue and brain burrito"?); a "good bargain if you don't mind the depressing Southwest decor", it's a popular hangout for the local mountain bike crowd; critics complain that "noise is the main dish."

Cadillac Bar & Restaurant/LS ⎣14 ⎜14 ⎜13 ⎜$19⎦
1 Holland Court (bet. Howard & 4th Sts.), 543-8226
*M – Possibly the "noisiest restaurant in the universe",
this SOMA Mexican "barn and grill" is "popular with
gringo yuppies" in the mood "to drink and get loud";
though some praise the fajitas and mesquite-grilled fish,
others call the food "microwavey" and "second-rate" –
but you "go there for the fun, not the food"; "bring a
bullhorn" or forget about talking.*

CAFE AT CHEZ PANISSE/LM ⎣25 ⎜19 ⎜20 ⎜$26⎦
1517 Shattuck Ave. (bet. Cedar & Vine Sts.), Berkeley,
548-5049
*U – "As much fun as its big sister downstairs" and "a
much better deal", say fans of Alice Waters' casual
upstairs California-Italian; "wonderful" pizzas, calzones
and pastas and "heavenly" desserts are all "highly
original" and made from ingredients so fresh "you can
taste the life energy in them"; critics, say it's "nothing to
flip over" and complain of long waits, high prices and
"condescending" service.*

Cafe Claude/M ⎣19 ⎜17 ⎜14 ⎜$15⎦
7 Claude Lane (bet. Bush & Sutter Sts.), 392-3505
*U – The "closest thing to Paris" in the Financial
District, this "tres francais" bistro provides "tasty bar
food" and a nice "European ambiance" at "very
reasonable" prices; it's "very cramped" and the "lunch
din can be overwhelming", but most consider it a
"must for francophiles."*

Cafe De Bordeaux/SM ⎣ – ⎜ – ⎜ – ⎜ M ⎦
326 7th St. (bet. Harrison & Webster Sts.), Oakland,
891-2338
*Busy East Bay spot that offers Continental cuisine with
a hint of Chinese influence; some say it's "actually very
good for the price", but others claim the chefs are
"passing off Chinese food as French"; "usually very busy."*

Cafe Fanny/SMX ⎣21 ⎜12 ⎜13 ⎜$12⎦
1603 San Pablo Ave. (Cedar St.), Berkeley, 524-5447
*U – Alice Waters' "chichi stand-up" cafe gets high marks
for creative sandwiches and "the very best cafe latte";
some complain about the lack-of-chairs simplicity of the
place – "who wants to stand while eating? it might be
terrific in Paris, but not in a parking lot in Berkeley";
service can be "haughty" and prices are high, but most
feel the "delicious" food is worth the hassle.*

Cafe For All Seasons/SM | 20 | 15 | 17 | $19 |
150 W. Portal Ave. (bet. 14th Ave. & Vicente St.),
665-0900
50 E. 3rd Ave. (bet. El Camino St. & San Mateo Dr.),
San Mateo, 348-4996,
U – "Comfortable, unpretentious" neighborhood cafes
that offer "fresh and well-prepared" pastas, salads,
desserts and the like at "very reasonable" prices;
breakfast and brunch are especially popular; despite an
"unacceptable noise level and spotty service", most call
these identical eating places "stand-out bargains."

Cafe Greco* | 20 | 20 | 18 | $10 |
423 Columbus Ave. (Stockton St.), 397-6261
U – "Young, European-esque" North Beach coffee
house that offers "good java", "good atmosphere" and
"classical music" in a "knockout" room; it's "wonderful
for late-night coffee and dessert" or interesting people-
watching anytime; critics call it too "loud and trendy."

Cafe Majestic/S | 20 | 23 | 21 | $33 |
1500 Sutter St. (Gough St.), 776-6400
M – This "beautiful old Victorian" hotel dining room
gets raves for its looks ("a knockout", "one of the
prettiest in SF") and "Orient Express" atmosphere, but
mixed reviews for its California-Continental food
("solid" vs. "hit and miss", "outdated"); still, it's good
enough to be "a favorite for a romantic evening",
especially given the fine wine list and live piano music.

Cafe Mozart | 21 | 22 | 21 | $40 |
708 Bush St. (Powell St.), 391-8480
M – "Genuinely romantic" Downtowner offering rich
Continental food with a Viennese slant; "on a good
night, the food's superb – but it's not always a good
night"; still, the ambiance is "cozy and intimate" and
service is unobtrusive, making it "very nice for a special
occasion" or pre/post-theater; "a most civilized place."

Cafe Riggio/SM | 17 | 15 | 16 | $24 |
4112 Geary Blvd. (5th Ave.), 221-2114
M – Fans of this "bustling and popular" Richmond
Italian are willing to overlook its no reservations policy,
long waits and "cacophonous" noise level in order to
enjoy heaping portions of "simple but delicious" food
served in a "nice, homey" atmosphere; critics call the
food "ersatz", "cafeteria quality"; however, it must be
doing something right – it's always mobbed.

F	D	S	C

Cafe 222/SM

–	–	–	E

Hotel Nikko, 222 Mason St. (O'Farrell St.), 394-1111
*Attractive but cold Downtown hotel dining room
specializing in rotisserie foods and California cuisine;
some call it "excellent."*

Caffe Roma/LS

15	16	13	$16

414 Columbus Ave. (Vallejo St.), 391-8584
*U – "A great North Beach spot for people-watching",
this "molto Italiano" cafe features "angelic frescoes" on
the walls and a quiet, secluded terrace for passing the
hours in good weather; though some describe the food
as "cosi cosi", others praise the breakfasts, pizzas,
pastas, rich desserts and, of course, the coffee; service
is slow, but nobody's in a hurry.*

Caffe Sport/X

17	14	7	$25

574 Green St. (Columbus Ave.), 981-1251
*U – This boisterous North Beach Southern Italian gets
the Don Rickles award for "abusive" service by "surly
waiters who won't let you have it your way"; but that's
all part of the "fun" for fans who love the "huge
portions" of "garlicky Sicilian fare" and "gaudy",
"goofy" decor; others, however, call it "a total zoo"
and "only for masochists."*

Caffe Venezia/S

17	17	16	$19

1903 University Ave. (Martin Luther King Blvd.),
Berkeley, 849-4681
*M – "Cheap" and "very decent" homemade pasta
explains the crowds at this Berkeley Italian, a popular
student hangout; it's "not great" but it is "a good
bargain", with an "imaginative setting" and "friendly"
atmosphere; expect "very close quarters" and "noisy"
conditions at times.*

Cairo Cafe*

15	8	18	$18

104 Strawberry Village (Seminary Dr.), Mill Valley,
389-1101
*M – A Middle Eastern outpost in a Marin shopping center,
this "tiny" find offers "very unusual" and "authentic"
food, "friendly service" and reasonable prices, making
it a "good value"; belly dancers on weekends are an
attraction to some, a distraction to others.*

California Cafe Bar & Grill/S | 16 | 17 | 16 | $24 |
Village Shopping Ctr., 1736 Redwood Hwy., Corte
Madera, 924-2233
1540 N. California Blvd. (Civic St.), Walnut Creek,
938-9977
M – *Surveyors can't agree on this multi-location chain;
some say they offer* "good standard California cuisine"
in casual, "attractive surroundings"; *others call them*
"upscale yuppie Denny's" *serving* "fake" *food in*
"plastic" *settings; though locations vary in quality, odds
are you'll get a* "fair deal", *and the* "broad menu" *is
sure to have something to appeal to everyone.*

California Culinary Academy/M | 16 | 15 | 17 | $28 |
625 Polk St. (Turk St.), 771-3500
M – *Culinary roulette is the name of the game at this
Civic Center cooking school; as you'd expect, the food
is* "hit or miss" – "sometimes very good", *sometimes*
"ghastly" *and* "amateurish"; *ditto the service, but* "the
students deserve an 'A' for effort and watching them
makes for* "an entertaining evening"; *buffet nights are*
"not for those on a diet."

Cambodia House/SM | 23 | 16 | 20 | $17 |
5625 Geary Blvd. (20th Ave.), 668-5888
U – "Well above average" *and* "continuing to
improve", *this* "quiet and calm" *Richmond District
Cambodian offers* "wonderful food from Southeast Asia
without the usual tacky decor"; *don't miss the soup or
the* "great coconut sauces"; *service is* "attentive" *and*
"gracious" *and it's all a* "great value."

CAMPBELL HOUSE*/S | 28 | 24 | 26 | $34 |
106 E. Campbell Ave., Campbell, 408-374-5757
U – "Romantic" *South Bay spinoff of Le Mouton Noir
located in an* "old-style manor house"; *assets include*
"superb" *French-American cuisine, a* "cozy intimate"
setting and excellent service; devotees call it "a must!"

CAMPTON PLACE/SM | 25 | 26 | 25 | $46 |
340 Stockton St. (Sutter St.), 781-5155
U – *Chef Jan Birnbaum has kept this handsome hotel
dining room on top with* "superbly simple, classic but
inventive" *takes on haute California cuisine; breakfasts
are* "the best in SF", *and* "lunch and dinner are tops",
too; the setting is "elegant" *and hushed (*"the silence
was golden"*) and the service polished, making it a
potent power scene and* "one of the city's best special
occasion restaurants."

F	D	S	C

Cantina, The/LS | 12 | 16 | 15 |$19 |

651 E. Blithedale Ave. (bet. Lomita & Camino Alto Sts.),
Mill Valley, 381-1070

*M – "Cute" Marin Mexican "for a young, not hungry"
crowd – the gold-medallion wearing, moussed-hair
types looking for love; some call the food mediocre
Mexican "glop", others call it "good for an inexpensive
meal" – either way, the margaritas are "great" and it's
fun, lively and loud.*

Capp's Corner/SM | 16 | 12 | 15 |$17 |

1600 Powell St. (Green St.), 989-2589

*U – This "honest, unpretentious" Italian serves "good
family-style meals in a family kind of place"; you can
"eat yourself sick" on food "like Mama used to make"
while basking in a "red-checked tablecloth setting"; it's
"what North Beach used to be in the '50s", right down
to the "super jukebox" and the prices.*

Caprice, The/S | 15 | 23 | 17 |$35 |

2000 Paradise Dr. (Mar West St.), Tiburon, 435-3400

*U – "Why do grand views usually mean awful food?";
this Marin American-Continental is no exception – it
has "a magnificent panorama of SF from every table"
but "dull" food; "bring out-of-towners only."*

Caribbean Zone/LSM | – | – | – | M |

55 Natoma St. (1st St.), 541-9465

*Breezy, lively SOMA Caribbean with a real airplane
bar and waterfall; the food is iffy but the ambiance
more than makes up for any lapses; look for cheerful
service and moderate prices.*

Carlo's Restaurant/S | 20 | 18 | 19 |$20 |

1700 Fourth St. (G St.), San Rafael, 457-6252

*U – This funky Marin Northern Italian offers "different
and delicious" fare – "try Carlo's surprise"; prices are
moderate and the wine list ok.*

Carnelian Room/S | 15 | 25 | 19 |$40 |

Bank of America Bldg., 52nd Fl., 555 California St.
(Montgomery St.), 433-7500

*U – This "ritzy" Continental offers one of the city's top
views, but our surveyors "wish they'd hire a top chef"
to improve the "uninspired, hotel-like food" served by
slow "pretentious" waiters; some say "I could eat dog
biscuits with that view", others advise "have a drink
and leave."*

| F | D | S | C |

Carrera's/LSM | 22 | 16 | 18 | $16 |

1290 Powell St. (Doyle St.), Emeryville, 547-6763
*U – This "offbeat" East Bay Italian sleeper serves
"simple" good sandwiches, salads and other casual
trattoria fare at the counter or tables; the decor is
eclectic with lots of "interesting art work"; all in all, it's
"quite pleasant", and late hours make it a "great place
to stop in anytime."*

Casa Aguila | 23 | 15 | 19 | $17 |

1240 Noriega Ave. (bet. 19th & 20th Aves.), 661-5593
*U – "Wonderfully creative, healthy Mexican food" is the
main attraction at this popular Sunset District spot; "huge
portions" of fresh, "delicious", "bargain"-priced "unique
regional dishes", accompanied by "tasty sangria", are
served by a "pleasant, cheerful" staff; yes, it's crowded
and the waits are long, but it's "worth it" – besides, you
get a "second whole dinner in your doggie bag."*

Casablanca | 16 | 19 | 19 | $26 |

979 San Pablo Ave. (bet. Marin & Solano Aves.),
Albany, 525-2000
*M – East Bay "neighborhood favorite" with Persian food
and lots of ambiance; "it's like being in a Bogart film"
with good food and live piano music (play it again, Sam);
modest prices add to a "very pleasant" experience.*

Casa Madrona Restaurant/S | 19 | 24 | 19 | $34 |

801 Bridgeway, Sausalito, 331-5888
*M – Amazing! This Marin view restaurant actually has
decent food; on a nice night there's "no place prettier in
the Bay Area" and the California cuisine is "better than
average", usually "very good"; most of our reviewers
say it's "hard to beat" for the food-view combination.*

Castagnola's/SM | 12 | 15 | 12 | $27 |

286 Jefferson St. (Fisherman's Wharf), 776-5015
*M – "Touristy" seafood emporium that some say is
among the best of the Fisherman's Wharf lot, but others
blast for serving "overcooked", overpriced fish – "why
mistreat tourists?"*

Celadon/SM | 17 | 16 | 16 | $23 |

881 Clay St. (Stockton St.), 982-1168
*M – This Chinatown Cantonese gets high marks for its
"elegant" teakwood decor and "good dim sum", but
high prices cause some to declare "you can get better
food for less"; still, "if you must have decor with your
Chinese food", this is a good place to go.*

San Francisco

Cha Cha Cha's/LSMX
| – | – | – | I |

1805 Haight St. (Stanyan St.), 386-5758
This colorfully designed little restaurant, perfect for Haight Street, serves great spicy Cuban tapas and many different flavored fresh fruit sangrias; of course, the couple with purple-spiked hair may think it's expensive, but it's not.

Chambord/S
| 18 | 16 | 17 | $29 |

150 Kearny St. (Sutter St.), 434-3688
M – "A nice French cafe for the SF lunch crowd", this busy Downtown bistro provides good if somewhat "predictable" French-Continental fare in an "intimate" atmosphere; some complain that portions are small and overpriced, but its convenient Union Square location makes it a handy option.

Cheer's Cafe/SM
| 16 | 13 | 15 | $16 |

127 Clement St. (3rd Ave.), 387-6966
U – "Cheerful" Richmond District neighborhood cafe offering good pizzas, salads and sandwiches; most popular for breakfast and lunch, it's "simple" and "pleasant", especially when seated in the outdoor garden; prices are low but service can be a little spaced out – you may have to "trip the waiter to get any attention."

Chevys/SM
| 15 | 13 | 15 | $17 |

150 Fourth St. (Howard St.), 543-8060
650 Ellinwood Way (Contra Costa Dr.), Pleasanthill, 685-6651
302 Bon Air Shopping Ctr. (Sir Frances Drake), Greenbrae, 461-3203
M – "Fun, casual, kick-back-and-let-loose Tex-Mex chain that "does what it does well", i.e., provide decent Mexican food at reasonable prices in a "lively" setting with "lots of action"; some swear by the "terrific fajitas" and "addictive chips", others dismiss it as the "same ol' Americanized Mexican" fare.

CHEZ PANISSE
| 27 | 21 | 23 | $54 |

1517 Shattuck Ave. (bet. Cedar & Vine Sts.), Berkeley, 548-5525
M – The East Bay birthplace of California cuisine is still considered by many "the gold standard" against which all others are measured; Alice Waters turns "fantastic" fresh ingredients into innovative, "memorable" meals that her fans call "always a surprise, never a disappointment"; despite complaints about the no-choice menu and small portions at high prices, most pronounce it "as good as it gets", with "very friendly service" and a pleasant atmosphere.

China Moon Cafe | 23 | 14 | 18 | $29 |
639 Post St. (bet. Jones & Taylor Sts.), 775-4789
U – Reviews for Barbara Tropp's tiny Downtown "nouveau-Chinese" gem are virtually unanimous – the "unique" "East meets West" cuisine is "creative and delicious" and the cramped seating is "the most uncomfortable in SF", but most are willing to endure the pain for her "exotic", meticulous and "incredibly good" meals; service can be brusque and portions, like the chairs, are small – "you're hungry half an hour later."

China Pavilion/SM | – | – | – | M |
2050 Diamond Blvd. (bet. Willow Pass Rd. & Concord Ave.), Concord, 827-2212
East Bay Chinese that gets praise for plush decor and solid ratings for food and service; still, our surveyors keep their enthusiasm in bounds with no raves and some gripes, e.g., "ordinary" food; try it if nearby, but not worth a detour.

China Station/LSM | 11 | 14 | 12 | $17 |
700 University St. (3rd St.), Berkeley, 548-7880
M – What's "decent and cheap" Cantonese fare to some is "dismal" and "bland" to others, but long hours, a huge menu and easy parking make this a popular college hangout and "good late-night spot"; service is "indifferent" and decor "needs refurbishing."

Christophe/SM | 19 | 18 | 19 | $31 |
1919 Bridgeway St. (Spring St.), Sausalito, 332-9244
U – "Wonderfully intimate" French bistro that serves good food in a pleasant setting that's "snug as a sailboat's cabin"; though service can be "snippy", it's usually fine; most call Christophe a "find" and possibly "the last remaining decent French place in Marin."

Christopher's /S | 19 | 15 | 17 | $25 |
1843 Solano Ave. (Colusa Ave.), Berkeley, 526-9444
M – "Young, lively, inventive" East Bay Californian with an "interesting, sometimes daring menu" featuring Thai touches; "some dishes are excellent, others a disaster", but a "great view", "nice artwork" and good wine list help compensate for the misses; it's popular enough to produce high noise levels and long waits for tables.

Chu Lin*/S | 19 | 9 | 16 | $16 |
2428 Clement St. (bet. 25th & 26th Aves.), 668-6266
*M – The decor may be nonexistent and service
sometimes "somber", but this Richmond
Mandarin-Szechuan gets high marks for "very
authentic" food; don't miss the stuffed chicken wings,
fried eggplant and "terrific noodles"; it's been around a
while and fans say it's "always good."*

Circolo/LS | 20 | 20 | 18 | $27 |
161 Sutter St. (off Kearny St.), 362-0404
*M – "A good buy for a luxury place", this upscale
Downtown Italian offers "very good food" and a
"snazzy" setting at prices that are "inexpensive for the
area"; it's "always crowded at lunch time" and, hence,
"noisy", but quieter and more relaxed at dinner;
service can be "slow" and "snobbish."*

Citrus North African Grill/S | 19 | 14 | 19 | $21 |
2373 Chestnut St. (Scott St.), 563-7720
*U – "Gracious" Marina North African serving "great
Moroccan food that you don't have to eat with your
hands"; the "menu is limited but everything is delicious",
including top-flight couscous, good lamb and great
apple pie; garden seating is a plus, as are modest prices.*

City Block/M | 22 | 18 | 18 | $30 |
101B South Park (bet. 2nd & 3rd Aves.), 543-3663
*M – The "extremely imaginative" California cuisine
served at this SOMA spot doesn't always work, but
when it does it's "different", "exotic" and "wonderful" –
"try the fried won ton and sashimi appetizer"; some
find the "very LA" post-industrial decor "a bit spartan",
but overall most call this a "winner" – "tough to find
but worth the visit."*

Clement Street Bar & Grill/S | 17 | 15 | 17 | $20 |
708 Clement St. (8th Ave.), 386-2200
*U – An "old standby", this "comfortable and reliable"
Richmond neighborhood pub offers "simple American
food at a decent price"; burgers, salads and fish are
"always satisfying" and the atmosphere is "warm" and
cozy, with a fireplace that's "inviting on a rainy day."*

Cliff House/LSM | 13 | 21 | 15 | $23 |
1090 Point Lobos Ave. (Great Hwy.), 386-3330
*U – This Richmond "tourist attraction" is best for
cocktails while savoring "tremendous" waterfront sights,
but "say sayonara" and dine elsewhere because "you
can't eat the view" and the American food is merely
"average" at best; brunch is a safe bet.*

Cordon Bleu Vietnamese*/SM | 21 | 10 | 16 | $14 |
1574 California St. (Polk St.), 673-5637
*U – "Amazing food at an amazing price" makes this
bargain Vietnamese in the Van Ness-Polk area one of
the city's most popular Asians; BBQ chicken is singled
out for praise; don't look for much in the way of decor
or service, but with food this tasty, who cares?*

Corona Bar & Grill/SM | 20 | 20 | 18 | $25 |
88 Cyril Magnin (Ellis St.), 392-5500
*M – "Trendy, upscale" Downtown Cal-Mex that gets
high marks for its "zippy flavors", "slick" looks and
"jumping" atmosphere; don't miss the quesadillas,
seafood burritos and fresh margaritas; "vacuous
service" and high noise levels are minuses, moderate
prices a plus.*

Courtyard, The/SM | 15 | 18 | 17 | $22 |
2436 Clement St. (25th Ave.), 387-7616
*U – "Relaxed and airy" Richmond neighborhood
American with food that ranges from "average" to
"quite good"; "unpretentious" ambiance and
"friendly" service are pluses.*

Cuba/SM | 13 | 5 | 11 | $15 |
2886 16th St. (S. Van Ness Ave.), 864-9871
*U – With one of the Survey's lowest decor ratings, this
affordable Mission District Caribbean is unarguably a
dump, but there's a dispute as to whether it serves
"simple, authentic Cuban food" or "forgettable" fare
that "doesn't taste like" the real thing.*

Curbside Cafe/S | – | – | – | I |
2417 California St. (Fillmore St.), 929-9030
*Teeny Pacific Heights storefront that caters to a tony
clientele with "good breakfasts"; usually crowded, but
service is friendly and there's a congenial feeling of
shared experience here; "if there's a smaller place in
town, it must be a shoebox."*

Dal Baffo | 22 | 20 | 23 | $40 |
878 Santa Cruz Ave. (University Dr.), Menlo Park,
325-1588
*M – "Pricey" Peninsula Continental that provides
generally good French-Italian cuisine accompanied by a
"terrific wine list"; some find the men's club setting
"pretty stiff" and service "stuffy", but most call it a
"credible upscale performer."*

| F | D | S | C |

DePaula's Restaurant and Pizzeria/LSM

| 16 | 12 | 15 | $19 |

1529 Fillmore St. (bet. Geary & O'Farrell), 346-9888
*U – An eclectic combination of pizza and Brazilian food
sets this modest Pacific Heights place apart; the pizza
("contender for best in SF") gets higher marks than the
South American fare ("Brazilian dishes are bland"), but
customers like the upbeat ambiance; calling it a "nice
local hangout."*

Diamond Street Restaurant/SM

| 17 | 11 | 18 | $19 |

737 Diamond St. (24th St.), 285-6988
*M – Experience a '60s flashback at this "low-key" Noe
Valley semi-vegetarian; "you just feel healthy" digging
into walnut spinach lasagna and other "wholesome",
"delicious" and "inexpensive" fare; some dishes aren't
as successful, but the laid-back atmosphere and
"excellent" service make up for minimal decor.*

Dipsea Cafe

| 17 | 14 | 14 | $13 |

1 El Paseo Ctr. (Sunnyside), Mill Valley, 381-0298
*U – "The true Mill Valley hangout", this clubby
cafeteria-style spot specializes in delicious breakfasts
and "down-home" lunches; "great pancakes" and
other tasty homemade goodies make this a favorite
with the local power breakfast crowd and carbo-loading
distance runners; service is "a little too mellow" for some.*

Doidge's Kitchen/SM

| 21 | 13 | 16 | $16 |

2217 Union St. (Fillmore St.), 921-2149
*U – "A SF tradition", this crowded, noisy spot is home
of the definitive AM power scene; "if breakfasts were
cars this one would be a Mercedes", with great French
toast, waffles, bacon and eggs "like your mother made";
lunchtime burgers and soups are less successful; having
to make reservations for breakfast and to endure
"rude" service puts some off.*

DONATELLO/SM

| 24 | 24 | 24 | $47 |

Donatello Hotel, 501 Post St. (Mason St.), 441-7182
*U – Considered one of the "best Northern Italians in
SF" by many, this formal Downtowner earns lavish
praise for its "outstanding" cuisine, "impeccable"
service and "luxurious yet unstuffy atmosphere" –
"class all the way", "always a pleasurable experience";
though a few critics ask "how do you say 'overrated' in
Italian?", most dub it "a place not to miss – save your
money for this one."*

Don Ramon's Mexican | 12 | 15 | 16 | $17 |
Restaurant/S
225 11th St. (bet. Howard & Folsom Sts.), 864-2700
M – Fans of this Mission area Mexican praise its "huge portions" of "always reliable" food and "great margaritas"; critics say "no way, Jose" and point to "boring", "Americanized" fare; friendly service and low prices help decide the battle.

Doug's BBQ/LSMX | 21 | 3 | 12 | $12 |
3600 San Pablo Ave. (36th St.), Emeryville, 655-9048
M – Some of the "best BBQ in the Bay Area" can be had at this inexpensive East Bay dump; fans call it "incredibly tender and tasty", with unusual meats like goat and turkey along with the more familiar varieties; forget about decor – "get it and eat it at home" if you want something to look at.

Dusit Thai* | 23 | 15 | 19 | $14 |
3221 Mission St. (Valencia), 826-4639
U – "Tastefully presented Thai food" earns high marks for this Mission Asian; it's a "neighborhood place that does not disappoint", with "wonderful flavors", "excellent service" and "reasonable prices"; try the squid sate and the iced coffee; "we've never had a bad dish."

Ebisu/SM | 23 | 15 | 20 | $19 |
1283 Ninth Ave. (Irving St.), 566-1770
U – Popular Sunset Japanese that offers "excellent sushi second only to Kabuto"; a "good variety of very fresh fish" comes in "creative and artistic" presentations; for the dedicated sushi-phile, "try the pokey hand roll"; with "friendly service", this is a local favorite.

Eddie Jacks/M | 20 | 18 | 18 | $28 |
1151 Folsom St. (bet. 7th & 8th Sts.), 626-2388
M – Trendy SOMA spot with "always innovative", but not always successful California grill food – "some weird food combos don't work but others are excellent"; "loud and crowded" with an "eclectic yuppie clientele", it features "neo-punk" decor and "great service from a knowledgeable staff."

Eddie Rickenbacher's | 16 | 17 | 15 | $21 |
133 Second St. (New Montgomery St.), 543-3498
U – Funky SOMA World War I theme restaurant that specializes in "good burgers", salads and other casual American food; it's "cramped, noisy" and loud, but it's an "affable place" that's lots of fun; check out the shoestring potatoes.

Edokko/S | – | – | – | M |
2215 San Pablo Ave. (Old Stone Way), Berkeley,
841-9505
*East Bay Japanese that some call a "cheap and
satisfying family restaurant", but others call "a joke"
with "nasty service and poor food"; there are many
better in the Bay Area.*

El Drisco Hotel*/S | 19 | 23 | 21 | $26 |
El Drisco Hotel, 2901 Pacific Ave. (Broderick), 346-2880
*U – A pleasant discovery in a Pacific Heights residential
area, this "elegant and romantic hideaway" serves
traditional, surprisingly good English-American food;
"terribly proper" with "wonderful atmosphere", you
can take your girl or your granny.*

Elite Cafe, The/SM | 15 | 17 | 16 | $26 |
2049 Fillmore Ave. (bet. California & Pine), 346-8668
*M – Pacific Heights Cajun which some say is on a "slow
downward spiral"; though you can still enjoy some
spicy Southern specialties here, most call the food
"mediocre" and complain the "blackened items are so
burnt that you have to guess what they are"; still, it's
loud and crowded, and often has long waits for tables.*

El Paseo/SM | 20 | 24 | 22 | $35 |
17 Throckmorton St., Mill Valley, 388-0741
*U – This Marin Continental draws more praise for its
"intimate and very romantic" atmosphere than for its
Continental food, which, though good, is somewhat
"old-fashioned" and "not memorable"; but given its
fine wine list and "one of the coziest rooms in town",
it's still a "great romantic hideaway spot."*

El Sombrero/S | 15 | 15 | 16 | $18 |
5800 Geary Blvd. (22nd Ave.), 221-2382
*M – Some say this Mission District Mexican serves
"huge portions" of "consistently good" food, including
"great handmade tortillas"; others say it serves "TV
dinner Mexican" that's "heavy and bland"; all agree
that service is friendly, the margaritas powerful and the
decor a bit "rundown."*

El Tapatio*/S | 13 | 14 | 16 | $17 |
475 Francisco St. (bet. Powell & Mason Sts.), 981-3018
*U – "Friendly family" Mexican in an odd bar-like
setting at Fisherman's Wharf; the food is "steady", but
margaritas and sangria are even better; can be noisy
and uncomfortable.*

F	D	S	C

El Tazumal Restaurant & | 16 | 9 | 16 | $15 |

Taqueria/LSM

3522 20th St. (Mission St.), 550-0935

M – Despite a sharp drop in food ratings, this Mission Salvadoran is still called "authentic", "cheap and good" by its fans, who praise the tongue and its other Latin American specialties; friendly service and low prices help make it a "good neighborhood joint", in a "dreary location."

Embarko | 19 | 21 | 17 | $27 |

100 Brannan St. (Embarcadero), 495-2120

U – Brand new SOMA yupperia offering trendy, but quite good modern American food; "potato pancakes to die for, excellent duck salad" and super burgers top the "imaginative" menu, which is enhanced by a great wine list; a "fun young atmosphere", "modern hip" decor and "friendly" service complete the "lively" picture.

Emerald Garden/SM | 21 | 20 | 19 | $19 |

1550 California St. (bet. Polk & Larkin Sts.), 673-1155

U – A "lovely little gem" in the Van Ness area offering French-influenced Vietnamese; the setting, food and service are all praised; prices are moderate.

Empress of China/SM | 16 | 18 | 16 | $26 |

838 Grant Ave. (bet. Clay & Washington Sts.), 434-1345

U – "Big, gaudy" Cantonese banquet place in Chinatown offering "overpriced, ordinary" food; good for tourists who have never had really good Chinese food", though even they won't like the "indifferent service"; "what with all the great Chinese places in SF, this one can be skipped without harm."

Enoteca Lanzone/LSM | 18 | 22 | 18 | $30 |

601 Van Ness Ave. (Opera Plaza, Golden Gate Ave.), 928-0400

M – Formerly known as Modesto Lanzone's, this reformatted Civic Center spot has a "beautiful art-filled setting" and Italian food that some call "very good", others call "very disappointing"; even if your meal is less than first-rate, you'll enjoy the "stunning" decor, "friendly" service and "great wine list."

Ernesto's/LSM | 19 | 13 | 19 | $18 |

2311 Clement St. (24th Ave.), 386-1446
U – "You must like garlic and have a big appetite" to
make the most of this down-to-earth Richmond
Southern Italian; it's a "perfect family dinner place",
with huge portions of "good earthy Italian food" at
"cheap" prices; it's also the "friendliest place in town"
and "they love kids", too.

ERNIE'S/SM | 22 | 24 | 23 | $50 |

847 Montgomery St. (bet. Pacific & Jackson Sts.),
397-5969
M – This SF tradition is earning praise after a
revamp – "once again in top form", with a new slant
on French food provided by a distinguished French
chef Alain Rondelli, who previously cooked at
France's Michelin three-star, L'Esperanee, and at the
Elysees Palace, for France's Presidents; most feel a
brighter look and Rondelli's cuisine are both working
well; the "personable staff" and excellent wine list
are extra pluses.

Etrusca/SM | 21 | 26 | 21 | $35 |

121 Spear St. (Mission St.), 777-0330
U – "Solid" Northern Italian newcomer near the
Downtown waterfront with potential to be a major star;
so far the "gorgeous" decor far outshines the uneven
menu, which has some winners ("awesome desserts"
and "excellent pastas"), but other dishes "need work" –
as does the service; "give them time and they will
shine", say supporters; live piano music is a nice extra.

Fat Apple's/SMX | 18 | 13 | 16 | $13 |

7525 Fairmont Ave. (Colusa St.), El Cerrito, 528-3433
1346 Martin Luther King Blvd. (Rose St.), Berkeley,
526-2260
U – "Wonderful burgers", "great breakfasts", apple
pies and pastries "like your mom or grandmom made"
explain the lines outside these East Bay haunts; it's
"clean and neat", with "fast service" and a low-key
atmosphere, but dieters beware.

Faz Restaurant and Bar/LSM | 19 | 14 | 16 | $24 |

132 Bush St. (bet. Sansome & Battery Sts.), 362-4484
M – "Lively" Financial District American luncheonette
that specializes in smoked meats and fish; fans call it
"really different", with "great grilled meats" and BBQ
chicken; detractors call it "nothing special", "frenetic and
cramped"; it's "not bad for a casual lunch Downtown."

| F | D | S | C |

Feng Nian*/SM

| 19 | 12 | 20 | $17 |

2650 Bridgeway St., Sausalito, 331-5300
U – Decent but uninspiring Marin Mandarin that's "never awful, never great", offering a large selection of dishes in an unremarkable setting; satisfactory service and moderate prices are pluses.

Fior d'Italia/SM

| 15 | 16 | 16 | $28 |

601 Union St. (Stockton St.), 986-1886
M – North Beach institution that provides "Italian food as it was in the '50s", which pleases its fans and sets off its critics; some call it "solid, old-fashioned Italian-American" fare, others call it "passe and uneventful"; the "old-style decor" comes complete with fountain, and the "pushy" waiters in tuxedos are "classics."

565 Clay

| 16 | 15 | 16 | $27 |

565 Clay St. (Columbus Ave.), 434-2345
M – Some say this semi-vegetarian Downtowner provides "excellent grilled fish and sauces", "great fresh vegetables" and other "fresh, light and delicious food" in a "comfortable", "low-key atmosphere"; others say you'll endure "long waits" for "boring", "mediocre" food; the consensus is it's better for lunch than dinner and you certainly won't feel guilty after dining here.

Flea Street Cafe

| 21 | 18 | 20 | $27 |

3607 Alameda de las Pulgas (Avy St.), Menlo Park, 854-1226
M – "Be prepared to experiment" at this California-American health food spot on the Peninsula; it provides highly "imaginative" (some say "bizarre"), "fresh, fresh, fresh" food utilizing organic herbs and vegetables; to some it's "wonderful" and "unique", to others "precious" and "confused"; a "cozy" and "quaint" "ladies' tearoom atmosphere" and laid-back service complete the "straight from the '60s" picture.

FLEUR DE LYS

| 27 | 27 | 25 | $56 |

777 Sutter St. (bet. Taylor & Jones Sts.), 673-7779
U – "La creme de la creme" and the "hautest of the haute", this "exquisite" Downtowner is the Bay Area's best French; chef-co-owner Hubert Keller (formerly of the 3-star Auberge de l'Ill in Alsace) turns out delectable, "lush" creations that are "rich and rewarding"; "impeccable" service, a "posh" setting and excellent wine list complete the "superb dining experience"; it's "close to perfect in every way."

Flower Lounge/LSM | 23 | 17 | 17 | $23 |
1671 El Camino Real (Park Place), Milbrae, 588-9972
51 Milbrae Ave. (El Camino Rd.), Milbrae, 878-8108
5322 Geary Blvd. (bet. 17th & 18th Aves.), 668-8998
*U – Peninsula Hong Kong Chinese that opened a
branch this year in Richmond; crowds at all three lead
to a "madhouse atmosphere", but reviewers say this is
"the best Chinese food in town – by far"; at lunch there
is "superb dim sum"; the rest of the menu is exotic,
authentic, beautifully prepared and pricey, featuring
"wonderful seafood dishes"; decor is negligible.*

Flying Saucer/SMX | – | – | – | M |
1000 Guerrero St. (22nd St.), 641-9955
*An overnight success that has attracted wide attention
for its Eclectic, nightly-changing menu that tries to
impress and usually succeeds; French-California "with
attitude"; it's a moderately priced, slick, modern bistro
in the outer-Mission.*

Flynn's Landing/SM | 11 | 14 | 13 | $21 |
303 Johnson St. (Bridgeway St.), Sausalito, 332-0131
*U – The Sausalito harbor view isn't enough to save this
seafood restaurant from dropping precipitously in the
ratings; "drink here, but don't eat" seems to be the
prevailing sentiment; attractive nautical ambiance and
moderate prices are pluses.*

Fly Trap Restaurant | 19 | 20 | 19 | $28 |
606 Folsom St. (2nd St.), 243-0580
*U – SOMA American-Continental with saloon overtones;
most praise the "good, fresh California cuisine", "simple
elegant" decor and "creative, pleasant atmosphere" –
"this place feels like San Francisco"; pasta, fish, burgers
and soups win nods, as does the oddball name.*

FOG CITY DINER/LSM | 21 | 22 | 17 | $27 |
1300 Battery St. (Lombard St.), 982-2000
*M – "Still creative after all these years" but "easier to
get into now", Cindy Pawlcyn's glitzy, upscale
Embarcadero diner continues to turn out "exciting"
and "inventive" food in a "casually elegant, brash"
atmosphere; it's "great fun to graze" on the terrific
appetizer plates, though "all those little tastings can add
up to $$$"; despite complaints about noise and snippy
servers, this SF original has been paid the "supreme
compliment – copied in every other city."*

Fook, The | 16 | 10 | 12 | $14 |
332 Clement St. (4th Ave.), 668-8070
M – Richmond District no-decor Chinese that gets
praise for its inexpensive "good dim sum", but receives
considerable heat for being "greasy and sloppy" with
bonehead service; and what's a fook?

Fountain Court | 19 | 17 | 18 | $18 |
354 Clement St. (5th Ave.), 668-1100
U – A "very good selection of Shanghai dishes at
reasonable prices" can be had at this Richmond District
Chinese with stylish, modern decor; try the "excellent
moo shu pork", but get ready for "s...l...o...w service."

FOURNOU'S OVEN/LSM | 22 | 23 | 23 | $43 |
Stanford Court Hotel, 905 California St. (Powell St.),
989-1910
U – Nob Hill standby that's making a slow but steady
comeback under chef Lawrence Vito; oven-roasted
meats are the specialty and surveyors particularly love
the "wonderful lamb chops" and "exquisite roast
lamb"; the setting has always been "lovely" and service
shows "improved attitude"; with a "fabulous wine list",
this is on its way to again being a "SF treat."

FOURTH STREET GRILL/SM | 21 | 19 | 18 | $28 |
1820 Fourth St. (Hearst St.), Berkeley, 849-0526
U – Sunny, popular East Bay Southwest-Californian
that seems to be creating a new style all its own that
features "lots of energy and lots of spice"; surveyors
rave about its "exciting, fresh" cuisine, singling out
the sausages, salads and fish soup; service is friendly,
the atmosphere "warm and inviting" and the style –
very laid-back.

Franco's | 16 | 14 | 15 | $27 |
1912 Lombard St. (Buchanan St.), 929-9595
M – Old-style Marina Italian where the heavy food
matches the heavy environment; fans say it's "small
and intimate", with "very good food" and some of the
"best pasta in town"; critics say it's "bad enough to
stop one from ever eating Italian again"; pricey for
what it is.

FRENCH ROOM, THE/SM　| 25 | 27 | 24 | $47 |

Four Seasons Clift Hotel, 495 Geary Blvd. (Taylor St.),
775-4700

U – "Grand" Downtown dining room that offers
"modern food in a traditional decor"; reviewers love
the "gorgeous", "classy atmosphere" and the
"faultless" California cuisine of chef Kelly Mills; there's
low-cal "alternate cuisine" and a fine wine list as well;
all in all, it's "one of the best hotel restaurants in SF."

Gaylord Indian Restaurant/SM　| 18 | 20 | 16 | $30 |

Ghirardelli Sq., 900 North Point St. (bet. Polk & Larkin
Sts.), 771-8822

1 Embarcadero Ctr. (bet. Sacramento & Battery Sts.),
397-7775

317 Stanford Shopping Ctr. (El Camino Rd.), 326-8761

M – Surveyors seem to either love or hate this trio of
pricey North Indian restaurants; admirers praise the
"elegant, carefully prepared" food, especially the
"wonderful tandoori and curries"; detractors say "all
the food tastes the same and is loaded with grease";
as for the waiters, "boy, can they ignore you"; the
Ghirardelli Square location has "great views", but
you pay for them.

Gertie's Chesapeake　　| 19 | 16 | 18 | $25 |
Bay Cafe/SM

1919 Addison St. (Martin Luther King Blvd.), Berkeley,
841-2722

U – East Bay seafood hangout that offers lots of noise
and "wonderful" crab cakes, along with other "very
fresh and well-prepared seafood"; it's usually crowded,
but the ambiance is relaxed.

Geva's/SM　　　　　　| 19 | 20 | 19 | $23 |

482A Hayes St. (bet. Octavia & Gough Sts.), 863-1220

U – New Downtown spot featuring "terrific Caribbean
food" and a "very upbeat atmosphere"; though some
dishes are less successful than others, there's "plenty of
heart and soul in the cooking"; look for the interesting
vegetarian dishes and homemade breads; service can
be a little "lackadaisical", but "you'll feel like you're in
Jamaica" here, especially out in the garden.

Giramonti/SM　　　　　| 21 | 17 | 18 | $29 |

655 Redwood Hwy. (Seminary Dr.), Mill Valley, 383-3000

U – Popular Marin Italian that's the sister restaurant to
Adriana's in San Rafael; the food is "homestyle
Southern Italian" and stays good even when Adriana
Giramonti isn't around – try the antipasti and the
scampi; some complain about the service, but the view
is good recompense.

F	D	S	C

Golden Phoenix/SM

–	–	–	M

728 Washington St. (bet. Grant & Kearny Aves.),
989-4400
Big Chinatown family restaurant that seems to be
improving; although it's not going to win any beauty
contests (or culinary contests, for that matter), you
won't be wasting your time here.

Golden Turtle/SM

20	17	19	$23

2211 Van Ness Ave. (bet. Broadway & Valley Rd.),
441-4419
308 Fifth Ave. (bet. Geary & Clement), 221-5285
U – These attractive siblings serve "SF's best Vietnamese
in lovely surroundings"; the "imperial rolls are regally
good" and the service is "friendly" and patient; the Van
Ness branch is bigger and more attractive, while the
Fifth Avenue version is more intimate.

Goro's Robato

18	18	17	$21

591 Redwood Hwy. (Seminary Dr.), Mill Valley, 381-8400
M – "Good fresh sushi" and the "best Japanese
grill cooking in the area" help keep this Marin spot
popular despite small portions and sometimes
"abysmal" service; you'll find some "very good and
unusual" items on the menu, making for a "unique
Japanese experience."

GREEN'S/S

24	22	19	$27

Fort Mason, Bldg. A (bet. Marina & Buchanan Sts.),
771-6222
U – This "vegetarian paradise" in a converted Bayside
army warehouse has become a national institution;
besides being "politically correct", the place is "a real
treat in this homogenized world", with fresh bread,
pastas, salads and sandwiches that "even a meateater
can love", qualifying as some of "the most inventive
fare in SF"; service can be a little condescending, but
the "smashing" decor and view make up for it.

Guaymas/LSM

18	22	16	$25

5 Main St. (Tiburon Blvd.), Tiburon, 435-6300
U – "Intriguing" and "creative" regional Mexican food
in a "spectacular" setting on the Marin waterfront; not
the same old enchilada, this restaurant provides
"interesting combinations" of "fresh ingredients" in a
"festive" atmosphere; with its outdoor patio, it's the
"perfect place on a sunny day" to sip margaritas and
savor "great views."

Guernica/SM
| 19 | 17 | 19 | $33 |

2009 Bridgeway St. (Spring St.), Sausalito, 332-1512
M – Despite rising prices, this modest Marin Basque is still recommended for "great" paella (order a day ahead) and other solid Spanish and French dishes; attractive decor and a "very relaxing" atmosphere help make it a "perfect after sailing" hangout.

Gulf Coast Oyster Bar & Seafood Restaurant/SM
| 19 | 12 | 17 | $24 |

736 Washington St. (8th St.), Oakland, 839-6950
U – Reviewers like this Cajun jewel in the rough; it's "the best kept secret in Oakland" thanks to "great oysters", "wonderful jambalaya and gumbo" and crawfish pie, plus "bread pudding that's too good to be true."

Hahn's Hibachi*/SMX
| 22 | 8 | 15 | $12 |

1710 Polk St. (Clay St.), 776-1095
3318 Steiner St. (bet. Lombard & Chestnut Sts.), 931-6284
U – Grilling your own food at the table "is always fun" at these inexpensive Korean BBQ spots; they provide "excellent, cheap healthy food" (don't miss the "great BBQ squid") in a no-frills setting; also popular for takeout.

Hamburger Mary's/LSM
| 14 | 15 | 11 | $15 |

1582 Folsom St. (12th St.), 626-5767
U – Welcome to "funk city"; this SOMA "retro-hip" punk dive is where you can get "the best burger ever served by a Mohawked waitress"; chili omelettes, fries and "outstanding Bloody Marys" are also popular, as is the "good ogling" and "electric", off-the-wall atmosphere; critics say it's "ok if you're 21 and on drugs or wish you were."

Harbor Village/SM
| 20 | 20 | 16 | $23 |

4 Embarcadero Center (Front St.), 781-8833
M – Here's a twist: this Embarcadero Center Cantonese serves "the best dim sum this side of Hong Kong" AND it's "gorgeous", with a spectacular view; service can be "indifferent", prices moderate to high and reviewers are less enthusiastic about the non-dim sum menu.

Hard Rock Cafe/LSM
| 11 | 18 | 12 | $18 |

1699 Van Ness Ave. (Sacramento St.), 885-1699
M – The SF version of these high-energy noise-athons has all the HRC virtues and vices; good burgers, chili and shakes, interesting rock memorabilia, earsplitting noise and "horrific" waits – "not for anyone over 14", "only with visitors, ear muffs and novocaine"; the above price doesn't include the HRC T-shirts you'll probably have to buy for everyone in your party.

| F | D | S | C |

Harpoon Louie's*

| 13 | 12 | 16 | $18 |

55 Stevenson St. (bet. Market & Mission Sts.), 543-3540
U – Yet another noisy burger bar, this one in SOMA
has "great burgers", friendly service and a "fun dive
atmosphere"; however, it's "not for vegetarians" or
sensitive noses – "wear a gas mask, it's smoky in there."

HARRIS' RESTAURANT/LSM

| 22 | 22 | 21 | $36 |

2100 Van Ness Ave. (Pacific Ave.), 673-1888
U – Surveyors have few beefs with SF's top steakhouse; a
"carnivore's delight", the "best steaks west of Kansas
City" served by a "solid, professional" staff in a
"clubby", "throwback to the 50s", wood-paneled
setting; some find it "sooo stiff and formal" and object
to the high tab, but to most it's "worth the price."

HAYES STREET GRILL/M

| 23 | 17 | 20 | $31 |

320 Hayes St. (Franklin St.), 863-5545
U – Civic Center "California bistro" that serves what
many surveyors consider the "best fish in town"; it's
"fresh", "fabulously prepared", accompanied by
scrumptious shoestring potatoes and capped off by
desserts including "creme brulee to die for"; the setting
is simple but attractive, and service, which has drawn
brickbats in the past, has "improved."

Helmand

| 25 | 20 | 22 | $21 |

430 Broadway (Kearny St.), 362-0641
U – Afghan food in Chinatown may sound
incongruous, but this "delightful newcomer" is a hit;
surveyors praise the "savory, intriguing" food (try the
spicy kufta and the grilled chicken) served in a
"tasteful, comfortable dining room", all at reasonable
prices; add a "very amiable" staff and you've got a
"great addition to the SF food scene."

Himalaya Restaurant and Sweets/SM

| – | – | – | I |

12469 San Pablo Ave. (Clinton), Richmond, 236-4148
Inexpensive East Bay North Indian with a homey
atmosphere and painfully slow service; though "very
spotty", the food is usually good enough to produce a
steady stream of patrons and long waits; decor is less
than minimal, but at these prices, who's looking?

Hong Kong Tea House/SMX | 21 | 12 | 12 | $14 |

835 Pacific Ave. (Stockton St.), 391-6365

U – A "great variety" of "authentic" dim sum still draws crowds to Chinatown's original dim sum palace; you can find food "as good in nicer surroundings" elsewhere, but that doesn't deter dumpling-loving hordes from keeping the barn-like space packed, especially on weekends; prices are low, service can be "indifferent."

Horizons/SM | 14 | 19 | 13 | $24 |

558 Bridgeway Ave., Sausalito, 331-3232

U – "Great", "exquisite", "terrific" – but those adjectives apply to the view, not the "dull, uninspired" California cuisine provided by this Sausalito tourist spot; "go for lunch", brunch or coffee, but dine elsewhere.

House of Nanking/X | 25 | 6 | 13 | $13 |

919 Kearny St. (bet. Jackson & Columbus), 421-1429

U – "Close your eyes" to the "horrible grungy decor" at this Chinatown Shanghai specialist and you'll enjoy "incomparable" food that's "cheap" to boot; raves include "a great find!", "genius chef" and "absolutely fantastic zingy flavors"; service can be "dictatorial", but you'll probably be glad you followed their orders.

House of Prime Rib/S | 22 | 17 | 21 | $30 |

1906 Van Ness Ave. (Washington St.), 885-4605

U – There's "no better prime rib in SF" than at this cozy, well-run beef emporium; "give those arteries something to cry about" with "reliably good", always "tasty" meat; service is "old-fashioned" and friendly, and prices surprisingly reasonable; don't miss the spinach – it's almost as famous as the ribs.

Hunan Restaurant/SM | 21 | 8 | 14 | $17 |

924 Sansome St. (Broadway), 956-7727

U – "Bring a 50-gallon jug of water" to quench the fire after tasting the "unusual flavors" that are the specialty at this "hot hot hot" edge-of-Chinatown Hunan spot; don't miss the "best Chinese chicken salad around" and "harvest pork that will blow your socks off"; in a "barn-like", "noisy as a sawmill" warehouse setting, the word service is "not applicable", but most say it's "still a wow"; a few critics call it "a shadow of its former self."

Hyde Street Bistro/SM | – | – | – | M |

1521 Hyde St. (Pacific St.), 441-7778

A small restaurant with a large following of regulars that range from "blue jeans to mink"; friendly service, moderate prices and an unusual combination of Austrian and Northern Italian cuisines served in a '60s diner atmosphere draws crowds.

I Fratelli/SM | – | – | – | M |
1896 Hyde St. (Green St.), 474-8240
This often bustling Italian trattoria has wonderful homemade pastas with light Northern Italian sauces; low prices and unpretentious decor keep this charming hangout packed with North Beach locals.

Il Fornaio/LSM | 21 | 23 | 18 | $27 |
1265 Battery St. (Greenwich St.), 986-0100
See South of San Francisco Alphabetical Directory.

Il Pirata* | 16 | 11 | 16 | $20 |
2007 16th St. (Portero Ave.), 626-1845
U – Unpretentious Potrero Hill Italian that serves "lots of food, very cheap"; the decor is dingy and the service no-frill, but the decent food makes it a favorite with "local working people."

Imperial Palace/LSM | 19 | 22 | 20 | $29 |
919 Grant Ave. (Washington St.), 982-4440
M – "Fancy Chinese food at high prices"; some call the fare at this Chinatown Cantonese "very good", others say "sweet, gluey, Americanized"; likewise, the imperial decor is "too fancy" for some – "give me some linoleum"; as ratings show, fans are in the majority here.

India House | 20 | 19 | 16 | $33 |
350 Jackson St. (Battery St.), 392-0744
U – Once upon a time this Downtown Indian was the best in town, but now it's "mediocre and not what it was"; curry dishes still draw praise and some love the "intimate", read dim, ambiance – "great for blind dates, it's so dark you can't see them."

Indian Oven/SM | 23 | 15 | 17 | $19 |
237 Fillmore St. (Haight St.), 626-1628
U – Haight-Ashbury Indian that gets high marks for "imaginative", "wonderfully aromatic" food; surveyors love the "great sauces" and tandoori cooking; the ambiance is simple but attractive and the greeting from hosts Irene and Leo is always warm; it's a "bargain" as well.

Iron Horse, The/SM | 15 | 14 | 17 | $28 |
19 Maiden Lane (bet. Geary & Post Sts.), 362-8133
U – Our reviewers note that this expensive "old Italian standby" needs "some serious updating"; however, its regulars still love its "handy Downtown location" and consider the overwhelming "dark, dark ambiance" part of the charm.

San Francisco

Ironwood Cafe/M
| 19 | 18 | 19 | $24 |

901 Cole St. (Carl St.), 664-0224
U – A "good consistent neighborhood restaurant" that provides "delicious, simply prepared" California-American food in a countrified Haight setting; "terrific fresh fish" and "great desserts" are standouts on the changing menu; though service "can be slow", most call it a "real find", with a relaxed feel.

Island Cafe/S
| 20 | 16 | 20 | $19 |

59 Tamal Vista (Lucky Dr.), Corte Madera, 924-6666
M – This moderately priced Marin health food spot is California all the way and organic to the max; most call it a "great spot for healthy, creative food" in a "pleasant island atmosphere"; try brunch, it's groovy.

Isobune Sushi/SM
| 18 | 17 | 17 | $18 |

1737 Post St. (Webster St.), 563-1030
1451 Burlingame Ave. (El Camino Rd.), Burlingame, 344-8433
M – Go fishing for sushi at these "unique" and entertaining Japanese spots, where you sit at the counter and pluck "very good" sushi off little boats as they float by; peak hours are preferable, since the dishes turn over quickly; at other times, some fish "look like they've been circling for weeks"; "fun for children", it's "a great place to introduce people to sushi."

Ivy's/LSM
| 18 | 18 | 19 | $27 |

398 Hayes St. (Gough St.), 626-3930
M – This Downtown Continental is a good second choice for pre-opera or symphony meals if you can't get into Hayes Street Grill; though some call the food "uneven" and "blah", others say it's "surprisingly good for a large inexpensive restaurant"; "friendly", "attentive" service and a "nice atmosphere" are pluses.

Izzy's Steak and Chop House/LSM
| 19 | 17 | 18 | $27 |

3345 Steiner St. (bet. Lombard & Chestnut), 563-0487
U – Marina District steak house "filled with locals who know a good buy when they eat one"; decent, reasonably priced steak, creamed spinach that "would make Popeye proud" and soft shell crabs all get raves; "friendly" service and "comfortable pub atmosphere" add appeal.

Jack's/SM | 19 | 16 | 18 | $32 |

615 Sacramento St. (bet. Montgomery & Kearny Sts.),
986-9854

M – *"The menu is the only thing that's older than the
waiters" at this expensive "low-key" Downtown
French-American "SF landmark" where little other
than price has changed since 1940; "go in knowing it's
staid and quirky and enjoy" old-fashioned food
including sole with shrimp, filet mignon and sand dabs;
"if you're known, service is excellent, if you're one of
the faceless masses, good luck"; the "old-time
three-piece suiters" enjoy the men's club atmosphere.*

Jackson Fillmore Trattoria/LS | 21 | 11 | 16 | $26 |

2506 Fillmore St. (bet. Jackson & Pacific Sts.), 346-5288

U – *This "pleasantly noisy and bustling" Pacific Heights
Italian is "everything a neighborhood trattoria should
be", with "very garlicky" and "usually very good"
Italian food, "helpful, friendly servers" and "great
character"; go early or expect waits; couples are often
asked to eat at the counter in this tiny place.*

Jade Villa/SM | 19 | 12 | 13 | $16 |

800 Broadway (8th St.), Oakland, 839-1688

U – *The "best dim sum in East Bay" can be found at
this large, bright and moderately priced Chinese; "the
multi-ethnic crowd enjoys" a wide variety of "authentic,
un-Americanized" dumplings and other "pretty good"
dishes, though some suspect "there's a secret menu"
for those who speak Chinese; come early on weekends
or be prepared for long lines.*

Janot's/M | 22 | 20 | 20 | $33 |

44 Campton Place (Stockton St.), 392-5373

U – *"France personified in SF", this "small, intimate
and friendly" Downtown brasserie has a "charming
Continental feel", as well as "dependable, first-quality"
food; favorites include steak frites and onion soup;
service is "flawless", but some find the cozy two-level
setting "somewhat cramped."*

Java Restaurant*/LSM | 15 | 8 | 15 | $14 |

417 Clement St. (bet. 5th & 6th Aves.), 752-1541

M – *Fans of this Richmond District Indonesian say it
serves "great spicy fries" and other unusual fare, critics
blast it as the "worst meal in SF" – low prices make it
painless to decide for yourself; don't expect much decor.*

Jin Jiang Kee Joon*/SM | 17 | 24 | 23 | $33 |
Anza Bldg., 433 Airport Blvd., Burlingame, 348-1122
*M – Peninsula Chinese near the airport with interesting
food; some say it's a "bad location for a very good
restaurant", while others call the food iffy – success or
failure depending on what you order; attractive decor, a
"lovely view" and efficient service count in its favor.*

Juan's Place/SM | 14 | 8 | 12 | $12 |
941 Carleton St. (9th St.), Berkeley, 845-6904
*M – "Fun Mexican dive" in the East Bay that has
"no-frills, just good food", if you don't mind "frozen
and canned ingredients" – and at these low prices,
most don't; it's often "noisy, busy and crowded",
especially when the college crowd is around.*

Julie's Supper Club/L | 15 | 18 | 14 | $22 |
1123 Folsom St. (7th St.), 861-0707
*U – A "great lively atmosphere", funky '50s supper
club with "George Jetson meets Elvis decor" and
deadly drinks ("order a wu-wu" or one of the "best
martinis in town") explain the appeal of this
"hyper-active" SOMA spot; despite "mediocre at best"
California-American food and service, it's "crowded to
the max" and hard to beat for sheer fun.*

Julius' Castle/SM | 15 | 22 | 17 | $40 |
302 Greenwich St. (Montgomery St.), 362-3042
*U – "If only the food were as good as the view", this
Continental perched high atop Telegraph Hill would be
a winner; instead, it's "another SF tourist trap" with
"mediocre", "overpriced food" and "snobby" waiters
for whom "customers are an intrusion and
inconvenience"; getting a table with a view is "an
interesting exercise in restaurant politics."*

Kabuto Sushi/LS | 24 | 13 | 19 | $26 |
5116 Geary Blvd. (15th Ave.), 752-5652
*U – "First-rate sushi from a real showman sushi
master" is provided at this Richmond Japanese; given
the "great selection" of "impeccably fresh fish" and the
"skillful and entertaining" way in which it's made,
patrons don't mind the dull decor and "unpredictable
service"; late hours are another plus.*

Kan's/SM | 16 | 16 | 16 | $31 |
708 Grant Ave. (Sacramento St.), 982-2388
*M – Touristy Chinatown Cantonese that's "living on the
legend" – "the kitchen closed long ago", but most
customers don't seem to notice; elegant but dull decor,
doddering service and high prices complete a
"disappointing" picture.*

Kansai/M
| 18 | 13 | 14 | $21 |

325 Sacramento St. (bet. Front & Battery Sts.), 392-2648
U – Comfortable Embarcadero Japanese that gets high marks for "great sushi" and a worth-a-try, multi-course kaiseki diner, but lukewarm reviews for the rest of the "adequate" but "undistinguished" fare; waiters can be rude – "worst lunchtime service I've ever had."

Khan Toke Thai House/SM
| 23 | 22 | 19 | $23 |

5937 Geary Blvd. (24th Ave.), 668-6654
M – Fans say this Richmond showplace still serves some of "the best Thai food in town", "authentic, satisfying" and spicy ("even the mild dishes demand several kleenexes"); its culinary virtues help compensate for "slow" service, ornate decor that "needs dusting" and sit-on-the-floor eating that's "not for the unathletic"; critics say it's "slipping" and is "now surpassed by others."

Kim's*/M
| 21 | 14 | 22 | $17 |

508 Presidio Ave. (bet. California & Pine Sts.), 923-1500
U – This comfortable Vietnamese-Continental in Pacific Heights could be the "most underrated restaurant in town" thanks to "excellent Vietnamese food in a nice setting", "what a bargain for a lovely meal"; service can be slow, but Kim's "sweet disposition" makes everybody feel welcome.

King Charcoal
BBQ House*/LSM
| 15 | 7 | 16 | $17 |

3741 Geary Blvd. (2nd Ave.), 387-9655
U – Inexpensive Richmond District authentic Korean where patrons grill their own meat at the table; good food, with crisp and spicy kimchee (Korean cabbage salad) and a "great assortment of pickles" as favorite accompaniments; not a favorite is the "too smokey" interior – don't make plans for afterwards, "you'll go home smelling like barbecue."

King of China/SM
| 17 | 10 | 11 | $15 |

939 Clement St. (11th Ave.), 668-2618
M – "Consistently good dim sum" draws crowds to this noisy, football field-sized Chinese banquet hall in the Richmond District; most love the dumplings, though they can be "greasy" – "pot stickers do the backstroke in oil here"; slapdash service is a minus, low prices a plus; "prepare to wait on weekends."

Kirala*/S | 23 | 15 | 14 | $21 |

2100 Ward St. (Shattuck Ave.), Berkeley, 549-3486
U – "The wait is long but worth it" at this East Bay
Japanese, which provides "excellent sushi" and "great
yakitori", along with robata-grilled delicacies and other
exotic and delicious treats; quality rules over quantity
("not very much food" for the price), but most call it
"some of the best Japanese food around"; decor is
"clean and simple", service ofttimes "chaotic."

Kirin/S | 19 | 9 | 19 | $17 |

6135 Geary Blvd. (25th Ave.), 752-2412
U – Ignore the formica decor and you'll enjoy exotic
Korean-Chinese treats at this Richmond District place;
standouts include hacked chicken with peanut sauce,
black bean crab, dry fried chicken and what could be
the best kimchee in the city, but "ask the waitresses for
the best items, they're not on the menu."

Korea House*/LSM | 18 | 11 | 10 | $20 |

1640 Post St. (Laguna St.), 563-1388
U – Japantown Korean with good, moderately priced
kimchee and hibachi cooking at the table; the
elemental decor is "simple but pleasant" but service
is "terribly slow."

Kuleto's /SM | 20 | 21 | 19 | $29 |

Villa Florence Hotel, 221 Powell St. (bet. Geary Blvd. &
O'Farrell St.), 397-7720
M – "Urbane", "bustling" Union Square Northern
Italian that gets unanimous praise for its "European"
feel, but mixed reviews for food; though some praise
the "wonderful" pastas, great mixed grills and breads,
others call the fare "boring" and "not very original";
likewise, service can be "friendly" or "disinterested";
still, its handy for pre-theater dining and there's a
"great bar scene", too.

La Bergerie | 20 | 17 | 20 | $23 |

4221 Geary Blvd. (6th Ave.), 387-3573
U – Competent French food at prices that make this small
Richmond District spot a candidate for "the best deal in
Classic French cuisine" with "exemplary" duckling and
"wonderful rack of lamb"; critics call the food
"forgettable" and say the place is in need of "updating."

Lafayette on Pacific/SM | 17 | 18 | 17 | $32 |
290 Pacific Ave. (Battery St.), 986-3366
*U – "Honest, unsung French bistro" offering "pleasant"
if "undistinguished" food in a tiny Downtown setting;
"splendid steamed mussels" and hazelnut soup are
standouts; crowded at lunch, it's a "find for dinner";
some complain of "rude" service.*

La Fiammetta Ristorante | 21 | 20 | 21 | $32 |
1701 Octavia St. (Bush St.), 474-5077
*M – Promising Pacific Heights newcomer that offers its
"yuppie-and-aristocrat" clientele "excellent pasta",
"wonderful gnocchi" and other generally well-received
Italian fare in a "romantic" and "intimate" setting;
critics blast "tiny portions at large prices."*

LA FOLIE/M | 26 | 21 | 24 | $46 |
2316 Polk St. (bet. Union & Green Sts.), 776-5577
*U – A candidate for "sleeper of the year", this
"charming and oh-so-French" restaurant in the Van
Ness-Polk area provides "outstanding, beautifully
presented haute cuisine" from chef Roland Passot; "this
is a gem", with "divine" tastes, caring service and a
"lovely, relaxed atmosphere"; while a few critics call
the food "overworked" ("always one too many
ingredients"), most pronounce it "one of the most
exciting restaurants in town"; prices are high, but
weekday prix fixe dinners are a good buy.*

LAGHI/S | – | – | – | M |
1801 Clement St. (19th Ave.), 386-6266
*This tiny Richmond District Northern Italian, owned by
the former chef from Modesto Lanzone, produces hearty,
delicious and original food, especially pastas and risotto;
add charming trattoria decor and friendly service and
you'll understand why reservations are a must.*

La Ginestra*/SX | 18 | 13 | 16 | $22 |
127 Throckmorton Ave. (Miller St.), Mill Valley, 388-0224
*M – A "Mill Valley locals' favorite", this classic, cheap
Marin Italian is a good Sunday-dinner-with-the-family
kind of place; pizza, scampi, gnocchi and special ravioli
are some of the best items on the menu; cramped and
loud, but consistent.*

F	D	S	C

Lalime's/M | 23 | 18 | 21 | $33 |

1329 Gilman St. (Nielson Ave.), Berkeley, 527-9838
M – "Inventive and fresh" California-French cuisine
served in a "lovely", "comfortable" East Bay setting;
since a move to new quarters, some say quality has
slipped and you "now pay more for less", though most
still praise the food, calling it "sublime, interesting" and
"very flavorful"; service is attentive but the room
"tends to be noisy."

La Mediterranee/SM | 19 | 14 | 16 | $16 |

2210 Fillmore St. (Sacramento St.), 921-2956
2936 College Ave. (Ashby Ave.), Berkeley, 540-7773
288 Noe St. (Market & 16th Sts.), 431-7210
U – These Middle Eastern outposts in Pacific Heights
and two other locations consistently provide "plentiful
portions" of "inexpensive food" that's not only
delectable, but also healthy and a "great change of
pace; for neophytes, the sampler plates are a good
introduction; the line can be long, but it's a nice wait on
a sunny day.

La Mere Duquesne/SM | 16 | 18 | 18 | $26 |

101 Shannon Alley (bet. Jones & Taylor Sts.), 776-7600
U – The traditional French food may be "uninspired",
but most consider this old-fashioned Downtown "work
horse" a "very good buy for the money"; besides
reasonably good food, it offers a "pretty" if a "bit
worn" setting and an "unpretentious" atmosphere;
"pre-theater service can be terse."

La Mexicana*/S | 22 | 3 | 16 | $12 |

3930 E. 14th St. (40th St.), Oakland, 533-8818
U – This inexpensive East Bay Mexican is described by
some simply as "yum! yum!", but be careful – the
"world's best tortillas" are served in one of the world's
worst neighborhoods; decor rating nears an all time low.

Lanzone Alexander/S | 19 | 20 | 22 | $29 |

65 Moraga Way (Brookwood St.), Orinda, 253-1322
U – "Cute" East Bay Italian that gets good ratings but
otherwise "uneven" notices; most reviewers love the
linguine with clams and say the owner is charming;
interesting art and friendly service also help make this
an "inviting neighborhood place."

	F	D	S	C

La Pergola/SM | 20 | 18 | 18 | $32 |

2060 Chestnut St. (Steiner St.), 563-4500
M – Marina Northern Italian that gets kudos for "tasty pasta", "killer risotto" and other "delicious" fare; reviewers praise the recent decor makeover, but some find service in the "small and intimate", sometimes "very noisy" and crowded, dining room not up to par.

La Petite Auberge/SM | 18 | 18 | 15 | $29 |

704 Fourth St. (Tamalpais Rd.), San Rafael, 456-5808
M – "Inconsistent but usually good" upscale Marin French in a "quaint setting"; though some call the food "fussy and old-fashioned", enough like it so that it's hard to get a table.

LARK CREEK INN, THE/SM | 26 | 25 | 23 | $37 |

234 Magnolia Ave. (Madrona Canyon Rd.), Larkspur, 924-7766
U – "Bradley Ogden has done it again along with partner Michael Dellar", offering his "creative and unique" approach to new American cuisine in a sunny Marin Victorian; it's "a pleasure in every way", with "inventive, delicious, fresh" tastes, an "exciting" American wine list and "lovely, "romantic-in-a-California-way" setting; the few complaints of uneven service are drowned out in a sea of praise for this "spectacular" restaurant.

La Roca Restaurant | 20 | 12 | 18 | $24 |

4288 24th St. (Douglas St.), 282-7780
M – "Excellent seafood" in "great spicy sauces" and "warm, friendly" service are the hallmarks of this moderately priced Mission District Salvadoran, which often has long lines thanks to its no-reservations policy; critics cite lack of variety and insist that "quality has gone downhill" recently; the nondescript decor is non appetite-whetting.

La Rocca's Oyster Bar/MX | 20 | 11 | 17 | $22 |

Laurel Village Shopping Ctr., 3519 California St. (Locust St.), 387-4100
M – "Fresha fisha" and a "great raw bar" are the main attractions at this Pacific Heights seafood bar, a smaller version of the Swan Oyster Depot; some find it "a bit too expensive", service can be brusque and the "grade school-like seats" are uncomfortable, so you might prefer to take out.

| | **F** | **D** | **S** | **C** |

La Rondalla/LSX

| | 11 | 12 | 12 | $14 |

901 Valencia St. (20th St.), 647-7474

U – "It's always Christmas" at this "zany" Mission Mexican, thanks to its "tacky" holiday light decor, but the food is certainly no gift – "worst in the U.S.", "they put American cheese on the beans – arrgh!"; still, "it's a lark late at night" – "go for the mariachis", the "fun bar" and the margaritas.

Lascaux/SM

| | 19 | 24 | 19 | $33 |

248 Sutter St. (Kearny St.), 391-1555

M – Dramatic Downtown French where the "fabulous" decor (its basement setting is decorated to look like the caves for which it's named) "competes with the food for attention" and usually wins; while the ambiance is praised as "romantic" and "warm", the "hit or miss" food has "never reached its potential"; still, spit-roasted meats, pastas and desserts are praised and live jazz is a plus; "no caveman ever had it this good."

La Taqueria/SMX

| | 23 | 9 | 13 | $9 |

2889 Mission St. (25th St.), 285-7117

U – Some of the "best tacos and burritos in the Bay Area" can be found at this cheap, delicious Mission Mexican; add agua frescas, fruit drinks made with fresh watermelon, canteloupe and strawberries, for "a treat" "worth going out of the way for", though given the "fast-food" decor and atmosphere, you might want to "do takeout and go to a park."

La Traviata

| | 20 | 18 | 21 | $24 |

2854 Mission St. (24th St.), 282-0500

U – "Hearty Italian" in the heart of the Mission; fans love the "wonderful" food ("don't miss the tortellini or the sweetbreads"), "always good" service and "inviting atmosphere", not to mention the moderate prices; recently re-opened after a fire, it's "still a winner" and the new wood ceiling adds "tremendous warmth and grace."

L'AVENUE /SM

| | 25 | 19 | 22 | $33 |

3854 Geary Blvd. (3rd Ave.), 386-1555

U – Downtown food and prices in a "classy" Richmond neighborhood bistro, with unanimous praise going to Nancy Oakes' "fabulously creative" California cuisine; the "inventive but not overly clever" menu changes daily and features "exquisite dishes" "you don't need a magnifying glass to see"; "friendly, accomodating" service and "a good wine list" help make this one an all-around winner.

LE CASTEL
| 25 | 23 | 25 | $47 |

3235 Sacramento St. (Presidio Ave.), 921-7115
*M – "Fine dining in an intimate atmosphere" is the
name of the game at this "very pricey" Pacific Heights
haute French; the "excellent" food, "personal" service
and a "lovely" and "quiet" setting make it a good
choice for "romance or that important business
dinner"; critics find it "stale" and "stuffy."*

Le Central/M
| 19 | 18 | 18 | $31 |

453 Bush St. (Kearny St.), 391-2233
*M – Onion soup, cassoulet and roast chicken with
pommes frites are favorites at this traditional Downtown
French bistro; "the mood, atmosphere and owner say
'France'", as does the sign telling diners how many
days the cassoulet has been cooking; a good wine list,
but barbs for noise, crowding and uppity attitude.*

Le Club/M
| 21 | 22 | 24 | $44 |

1250 Jones St. (Clay St.), 771-5400
*M – "Clubby" Nob Hill French that provides pricey
traditional cuisine with old-style sauces; fans call it
"intimate and excellent", with polished service and a
"distinguished" atmosphere; critics counter "pretentious
and dated" – "if you're into blue-haired ladies and
old-world stuffiness, this is the place."*

Le Cyrano/S
| 21 | 18 | 21 | $25 |

4134 Geary Blvd. (6th Ave.), 387-1090
*U – "Dependable", moderately priced Richmond
District French standby; "far from gourmet", it's
"nothing fancy, just good French food", with attentive
service and "pleasant atmosphere" part of the charm.*

Le Domino/M
| 20 | 18 | 20 | $30 |

2742 17th St. (Florida St.), 626-3095
*M – A "wonderful, moderately priced Classic French
restaurant located in a "great old house" in the Mission
near the Galleria Design Center; "way off the beaten
track, but worth finding" for good food and "corny but
romantic" atmosphere; "when the service is on, the
place is great."*

Lehr's Greenhouse/SM
| 11 | 17 | 13 | $27 |

740 Sutter St. (Taylor St.), 474-6478
*U – This unusual restaurant/florist shop is filled with
"wonderful flora" that you may find yourself tempted
to eat, since the "cafeteria food" is "just above edible";
while most find the greenhouse setting "pretty", some
say even that "seems a bit run-down" and "needs
upgrading"; service can be "attentive" or "invisible."*

Le Marquis* | 24 | 18 | 23 | $41 |
Plaza Shopping Ctr., 3524B Mt. Diablo Blvd., Lafayette,
284-4422
*U – Fancy haute French in an East Bay shopping mall;
"pricey but worth it" for "great food", excellent service
and fine wine list; you'd never expect to find something
this good in a location this bad.*

Le Metropole/S | 16 | 18 | 17 | $32 |
2271 Shattuck Ave. (bet. Bancroft & Kittridge Aves.),
Berkeley, 848-3080
*M – East Bay Country French with hunting lodge
ambiance and romantic fireside tables; "nothing exciting,
but a dependable old friend" to fans, "gloppy" over-
sauced food to critics; bring a good book – "you can wait
45 minutes to an hour between appetizer and entree."*

L'Entrecote de Paris/LSM | 18 | 17 | 17 | $29 |
2032 Union St. (Buchanan St.), 931-5006
230 California St. (bet. Battery & Front Sts.), 433-4000
*M – "Perfect pommes frites" is the main claim to fame
at these breezy bistros; steaks, burgers and salads are
also praised, but the rest of the menu varies "from fair
to good"; service can be "friendly and cheerful" or
"rude", but a "good jazz pianist" may take your mind
off shortcomings.*

Le Piano Zinc/LS | 21 | 18 | 18 | $35 |
708 14th St. (Market St.), 431-5266
*M – The piano's gone and prices are lower at this Noe
Valley French, and most reviewers like the changes –
the prices now match the "tasty" and "occasionally
inspired" classic bistro food; the "eclectic, romantic and
sophisticated" supper club decor in this "crowded,
noisy, but alive and fun" place allows for "everything
from jeans to tuxedos."*

L'Escargot/SM | 22 | 21 | 23 | $33 |
1809 Union St. (Octavia St.), 567-0222
*M – Patrons of this cozy Union Street French return again
and again for the "quiet and relaxed" atmosphere,
"always reliable" food and "special and friendly service";
it's nothing flashy, but "you're never disappointed" and
it's a "good value."*

Le St. Tropez | 23 | 21 | 21 | $37 |
126 Clement St. (2nd Ave.), 387-0408
*U – "Wonderful" food and a "cozy", "very romantic"
atmosphere are characteristics of this Richmond District
French spot; "for an elegant meal and first-class service",
this "best-kept secret in the Bay Area" is a bargain"; a
fireplace helps make this the perfect Valentine's Day spot.*

64

| F | D | S | C |

Leticia's/SM
| 13 | 13 | 15 | $19 |

2223 Market St. (bet. Sanchez & 15th Sts.), 621-0441
*M – "Great people-watching" and "good margaritas"
are the main reasons to visit this moderately priced
Castro Mexican; as for the food, some call it "tasty if a
bit commercialized", others call it "only fair" and "not
very authentic."*

Le Trou Restaurant Francais/X
| 22 | 16 | 21 | $34 |

1007 Guerrero St. (22nd St.), 550-8169
*U – Featuring "original, uneven", but mostly "very
good" cooking, this "homey" little Mission bistro is a
"civilized oasis" with a "simple but elegant" setting and
a "very gracious host"; critics complain of "small
portions at big prices" and note that service is
"occasionally uneven, but forgivable."*

Little City Antipasti Bar/LSM
| 20 | 17 | 16 | $24 |

673 Union St. (Powell St.), 434-2900
*U – The "delectable" antipasti served at this lively, read
"noisy", North Beach trattoria qualifies as some of the
"best appetizers in town" – "shrimp borrachos are
dynamite", "roast garlic and brie is not to be missed";
"go with a group of people" and have fun "grazing",
but entrees are only "so-so", so don't bring a big
appetite; critics complain "too many yuppies per sq. ft."*

Little Henry's/LSMX
| 15 | 7 | 15 | $12 |

955 Larkin St. (Post St.), 776-1757
339 Steiner St. (Columbus Ave.), 673-4407
*U – "You won't starve" and you certainly won't go broke
at these Chinese-run Tenderloin Italians; its "huge
portions" of "tasty" food are "good and cheap for fast
fill-ups"; while decor is seedy and the neighborhood
"crummy", "keep it in perspective and it's worth it."*

Little Italy/SM
| 18 | 14 | 15 | $20 |

4109 24th St. (Castro St.), 821-1515
*U – "There's nothing subtle" about this boisterous,
"garlic heaven" Castro Valley peasant Italian; the food
may be "heavy" and lacking "finesse", but fans praise
the "fabulous pastas" and "excellent ravioli"; "friendly"
if "sometimes slow" service, with appropriately
"homey" atmosphere.*

Little Joe's/SM | 17 | 10 | 15 | $18 |

523 Broadway (Columbus Ave.), 433-4343

*M – "More of an experience than a place to dine", this
"rowdy" and "playful" North Beach Italian dishes up
"lots of garlicky Italian food" in a suitably cozy
atmosphere; "come here after a three-day fast" and
you might be able to handle the "huge portions" of
what some call "disappointing" and "mediocre" food;
enough find it "cheap and good" to produce long lines.*

L'Olivier/M | 22 | 21 | 21 | $34 |

465 Davis Court (Jackson St.), 981-7824

*U – "A small gem of a restaurant hidden away in a
courtyard", this Embarcadero Classic French offers
"excellent" cuisine in a "lovely" and "relaxing" setting;
it's "wonderful and underrated", with "gracious"
service and well-spaced tables, it's a perfect place for
quiet business lunches; don't miss the "best creme
brulee this side of the Sea of Tranquility."*

London Wine Bar, The/M | 12 | 16 | 15 | $21 |

415 Sansome St. (Sacramento St.), 788-4811

*U – The "food is definitely an afterthought" at this
Downtown wine bar, which features over twenty wines
by the glass and a knowledgeable service staff; though
some find soups and salads fine for lunch, others say
the California food is "best forgotten", and suggest you
take your nourishment in liquid form.*

Long Life Vegi House*/SM | 14 | 4 | 13 | $13 |

2129 University Ave. (Shattuck Ave.), Berkeley, 845-6072

*M – Health nuts love the "yum-yum" food served at
this East Bay Chinese Vegetarian, praising its "fresh,
well-combined ingredients" and "really delicious mock
meat dishes"; the decor may be "ugly", but the "price
is right."*

Lori's Diner/LSMX | 12 | 15 | 13 | $13 |

336 Mason St. (Geary Blvd.), 392-8646

*M – Downtown diner with "fun '50s decor" that's best
after midnight, especially if you like loud rock, bright
lights and greasy food; though critics call the food
"inedible", breakfast, burgers and hot dogs are best
bets and "cheerful service is a plus."*

Los Chiles/M | – | – | – | I |

2 Embarcadero Ctr. (Front St.), 433-8656

*The "special beef burrito" at this cheapie Mexican is
"the best bargain in Embarcadero Center", but the rest
of the fare is "yuk"; service and ambiance are sorely
lacking, so if you must go, "take out."*

Lucca Ristorante*/SM | 17 | 13 | 17 | $24 |
24 Sunnyside Ave. (E. Blythedale Ave.), Mill Valley,
388-4467
U – Fans of this Mill Valley Italian are willing to overlook
"tiny", "cramped" quarters and "uncomfortable
booths" to enjoy good food and friendly service;
despite the discomfort, it's a "good value."

Lychee Garden*/SM | 21 | 14 | 13 | $18 |
1460 Powell St. (Broadway), 397-2290
U – Despite brusque service, our reviewers say this
moderately priced Chinatown Cantonese is worth the
hassle for some of the "best Cantonese in town", with
"great noodles" drawing particular praise; "service is
almost non-existent", though "you may get more
attention if you're Chinese."

MacArthur Park/SM | 18 | 18 | 17 | $25 |
607 Front St. (Jackson St.), 398-5700
M – Meat-eaters head for this moderately priced
Downtown grill for some of the "best ribs in town",
along with good chicken, salads, onion rings and the
like; head here for "fasten your seat belts" singles
action at the bar, "great simple meals" and "fun", even
if it's "damn noisy."

Mai's /S | 18 | 13 | 16 | $18 |
316 Clement St. (5th Ave.), 221-3046
1838 Union St. (Laguna St.), 921-2861
M – One of the first Vietnamese in town, if "their quality
pales compared to what's available now", this affordable,
"old standby" Richmond District spot maintains praise
for its soft shell crabs, "excellent shrimp and pork
rolls", rice noodle soup and imperial rolls.

Maltese Grill/M | 19 | 20 | 18 | $27 |
20 Annie Alley (Market St.), 777-1955
M – "Endearing play-it-again-Sam ambiance" sets the
tone at this moderately priced Mediterranean; though
"inconsistent", the food is mostly "tasty" and "fresh",
with paella, antipasti, lamb and "memorable garlic
chicken" singled out for special praise; service is
"friendly" and both portions and coffee cups are large.

Mama's/LSM | 16 | 13 | 14 | $20 |
398 Geary Blvd. (Mason St.), 433-0113
1701 Stockton St. (Filbert St.), 362-6421
U – Old-fashioned Italian-American coffee shops where
convenience is an asset; "let Mama serve you her great
breakfasts, but tell her you're not hungry for lunch or
dinner", since anything but the wake-up fare is
"wholesale and undistinguished."

Mama's Royal Cafe /SMX | 19 | 12 | 14 | $13 |
4012 Broadway (MacArthur Ave.), Oakland, 547-7600
U – "A blast from the '60s", this "weird little cafe" is
best known for "fabulous breakfasts" featuring "great
omelettes and hash browns", "excellent sausage" and
"creamy caffelatte"; service is "friendly but strange",
and decor "dingy" – "don't look too closely."

Mamounia/SM | 19 | 20 | 18 | $27 |
4411 Balboa St. (45th Ave.), 752-6566
U – Spend "an evening in another country", "pull up a
pillow" and use your fingers to eat the "tasty" North
African specialties at this moderately priced Moroccan
Disneyland in Richmond; critics complain that "portions
have shrunk" and "some dishes are excellent, others
just ok", but it's a "truly exotic" experience – "this is
how it feels to eat in the caliph's tent" – complete with
belly dancers.

Mandalay/SM | 23 | 15 | 19 | $17 |
4348 California St. (6th Ave.), 386-3895
U – A "little jewel", this Richmond District Burmese draws
all raves for its "wonderful", "unusual" fare – "don't tell
anyone about this", "outstanding food never misses",
"fish salad with garlic is to die for"; also try ginger salad,
curried prawns and fish fillets with black bean sauce;
decor is simple but attractive, service "courteous."

Mandarin House/S | 19 | 16 | 17 | $21 |
817 Francisco Blvd. W. (Balance St.), San Rafael,
492-1638
U – Is this the "best Chinese in Marin?"; it has a
"cheerful" atmosphere, highly touted food and
"great hosts", but some consider it "overrated" and a
trifle overpriced.

MANDARIN, THE/S | 22 | 23 | 19 | $35 |
Ghirardelli Sq., 900 North Point St. (bet. Polk & Larkin
Sts.), 673-8812
M – "Wonderful" Bay views and a "handsome",
comfortable setting set this pricey Ghirardelli Square
Chinese apart from the rest of the pack; it also has
"marvelous Chinese food, unfortunately at French
prices", prompting some to say "it's no longer worth
it"; the "specials are usually best."

| F | D | S | C |

Manora's Thai Cuisine/SM | 23 | 15 | 17 | $18 |
1600 Folsom St. (12th St.), 861-6224
3226 Mission St. (29th St.), 550-0856
*U – Among the best Thai restaurants in SF, these
Mission District and SOMA outposts serve "outstanding"
and "very reasonable" food featuring "fresh ingredients,
beautifully presented" – try red hot squid salad, yellow
curries and eggplant dishes; efficient service helps make
up for often crowded and noisy conditions.*

Marin Joe's/LS | 18 | 11 | 16 | $22 |
1585 Casa Buena Dr. (Tamalpais Dr.), Corte Madera,
924-2081
*U – "Still crowded after all these years", this hearty
Marin Italian can be relied on for a "good old-fashioned
meal" featuring tasty steaks and other grilled items at
reasonable prices; it's "not fancy", "waiting in the bar is
a pain" and the management can be "crotchety", but
"if you go more than twice you become family."*

Marrakech Moroccan | 17 | 21 | 18 | $30 |
Restaurant/SM
419 O'Farrell St. (Taylor St.), 776-6717
*M – This Downtown Moroccan is "good for a satisfying
fun dinner with a group", especially "if the belly dancer
puts on a fine show"; while it may not be the best meal in
town, it's entertaining and certainly not the same old thing.*

MASA'S | 28 | 25 | 27 | $66 |
648 Bush St. (Powell St.), 989-7154
*U – "The standard setter" and "exquisite in every
way", this "awesome" Nouvelle French once again
takes first place in the Survey's food ratings; chef Julian
Serrano's rich cuisine is an "always new and
interesting" "nirvana for the taste buds" – "if I had a
million dollars, I'd eat here every week"; the setting is
"supremely elegant" and service "impeccable"; though
a few feel it has "lost its magic", they're in a clear
minority, as the long wait for reservations proves.*

Max's Diner/LSM | 16 | 16 | 16 | $18 |
311 Third St. (Folsom St.), 546-0168
*M – Kitschy decor, friendly waitresses in bobby sox and
poodle skirts, and "huge portions of real diner food"
draw crowds to this "friendly" SOMA spot; Buffalo
wings, corned beef hash, grilled cheese and shakes are
typical of the "heavy but good", "truck-stop" fare;
critics say the "cuteness wears thin" and the food's just
"average", but long waits attest to Max's popularity.*

Max's Opera Cafe/LSM | 16 | 17 | 16 | $20 |
601 Van Ness Ave. (Golden Gate Ave.), 771-7300
*U – Late hours and a convenient Civic Center location
make this "upbeat" deli a good choice for a post-opera
or symphony bite, even if the "exquisitely sinful"
desserts are better than the "abundant but mediocre"
main dishes; singing waiters are either "fun" or
"off-key", depending on your musical standards.*

Maye's Oyster House/M | 15 | 12 | 17 | $25 |
1233 Polk St. (Bush St.), 474-7674
*U – "An oldie but still good", this moderately priced
Van Ness seafood house provides "old-fashioned,
simply prepared" fish in a dark woody setting that
could use some "spiffing up"; it's stuck in a "'40s time
warp, including the food", but that's ok by fans who
appreciate its "consistent quality and reasonable prices."*

Mekong*/SMX | 22 | 6 | 16 | $12 |
730 Larkin Ave. (O'Farrell St.), 928-8989
*U – This Tenderloin Vietnamese is a favorite thanks to
"very cheap, very good" food, even though the
bare-bones setting "could use a little style"; "go with a
group and try as many vegetable dishes as possible",
and don't miss the "great spring rolls" and specialty
soups; "friendly" service adds to the "great deal."*

Mela/SM | – | – | – | M |
417 O'Farrell St. (bet. Jones & Taylor Sts.), 776-7171
*"Unique Indian cuisine from Gujarat province" in an
attractive Downtown setting; the menu is "very
limited", but it "works" and portions are "tiny" but big
on taste thanks to "lots of good sauces."*

Mel's Diner/LSMX | 11 | 16 | 13 | $13 |
2165 Lombard St. (bet. Fillmore & Steiner), 921-3039
3355 Geary Blvd. (Spruce St.), 387-2244
*U – "Looks can be deceiving", as this retro diner
proves – it has "cute" '50s-style decor, but "lousy"
food; still, it's "ok for the under 18 set", and "where
else are you gonna go at 3:30 AM?"*

Mescolanza/M | 21 | 14 | 19 | $21 |
2221 Clement St. (23rd Ave.), 668-2221
*U – Small, "crowded but convivial" Richmond Italian
that's winning friends with "wonderful" pizzas, pastas,
veal dishes and other "just plain good" food at good
prices; don't miss the salad dressing – they bottle their own.*

Middle East Restaurant* | 15 | 12 | 18 | $18 |

2125 University Ave. (Shattuck), Berkeley, 549-1926
*U – "One of the better Middle Eastern places", this
East Bay spot wins mostly praise for its "good,
home-cooked food" and "small, intimate setting"; the
generous appetizer platter is a good introduction to this
"terrific low-cost alternative."*

Mifune/SM | 18 | 12 | 16 | $12 |

1737 Post St. (bet. Webster & Buchanan Sts.), 922-0337
*U – A favorite Japantown "noodle nook", this Tokyo-
style spot provides "fast, cheap and authentic" noodles
in a "huge variety of soups"; the formica decor is part
of the fun; "rent the video of Tampopo, then go here."*

Mikado*/SMX | 18 | 16 | 19 | $23 |

6228 Telegraph Ave. (63rd St.), Berkeley, 654-1000
*U – East Bay sushi and teriyaki spot that offers "good
food for a great price"; it's a "nice neighborhood
place", with understated decor and dutiful service.*

Mike's Chinese Cuisine/SM | 19 | 13 | 16 | $19 |

5145 Geary Blvd. (16th Ave.), 752-0120
*M – Fans of this Richmond Cantonese praise its "very
good" food ("try the cashew chicken") and "nice,
quiet" setting; critics say it "recalls 1950s Chinese food
for non-Chinese" – success here depends on "knowing
what to order."*

Milano Joe's/LSM | 18 | 15 | 18 | $21 |

1175 Folsom St. (7th St.), 861-2815
*M – "Loud and trendy" SOMA Italian that serves what
some call "surprisingly good" food (especially "great
pasta") but others dismiss as "forgettable"; it "jams in
the evening" with a lively after-work crowd.*

Milano Pizzeria/LMX | – | – | – | I |

1330 Ninth Ave. (Judah St.), 665-3773
*Popular Sunset District pizzeria with "very good" pies
at a good price; some claim the other menu items are
even "better than the pizza."*

Milly's*/SM | 16 | 14 | 16 | $19 |

1613 Fourth St. (F St.), San Rafael, 459-1601
*M – This Marin Vegetarian divides sprout lovers into two
camps: those who call it "excellent", with the "best red
cabbage and walnut salad in the world", and those who
call it "boring" – "this will make vegetarians go back to
meat"; quality seems to depend on "who's cooking
tonight"; look for "ersatz Southwest decor" and service.*

Mirabelle*/S | 22 | 18 | 20 | $27 |
1549 Shattuck Ave. (Cedar Ave.), Berkeley, 841-2002
*U – East Bay Continental bistro that wins raves for its
simple regional fare – "delightfully good food", "a
terrific value for the money"; the bouillabaise and
homemade pastries are singled out for special praise;
service is "attentive" but sometimes slow, and the
setting "intimate and cozy."*

Miss Pearl's Jam House/SM | 17 | 18 | 14 | $25 |
Phoenix Inn, 601 Eddy St. (Larkin St.), 775-5267
*M – "Hot style" and "hot food" have made this trendy
California-Caribbean "the newest hot spot"; though the
menu has "lots of hits and misses", the hits – like
"out-of-this-world jerk chicken" – are "worth fighting
the crowd for", and the misses don't seem so bad after
a few "monster drinks"; located in a "real '50s motel",
it has "fun decor" (including a pool) and a "funky",
loud atmosphere – you "must be under 30 to fit in."*

Miz Brown's Feed Bag/SM | 7 | 6 | 12 | $13 |
731 Clement St. (7th Ave.), 752-5017
3401 California St. (Laurel Village), 752-2039
1356 Polk St. (Pine St.), 771-4221
2565 Mission St. (bet. 21st & 22nd Sts.), 648-6070
*U – Richmond District greasy spoons that again receive
the distinction of coming in last in the food ratings; "it's
Denny's down two notches", with the "ambiance of a
truck-stop"; if you must eat here (i.e., if you're
"starved"), stick to breakfast.*

Moishe's Pipick*/MX | 15 | 7 | 13 | $14 |
425A Hayes St. (Gough St.), 431-2440
*M – This SF try for a good NYC-style deli doesn't cut
the mustard; this Civic Center spot "promises more
than it delivers" but some still hail it as "the closest
thing to a real Jewish deli in SF" and "the only place
for good corned beef."*

Mom Is Cooking/SMX | 22 | 5 | 9 | $13 |
1192 Geneva Ave. (Naples Ave.), 586-7000
*U – "Her place might not look like much, but Mom is a
genius at the stove", say fans of this "slightly shabby"
Mission Mexican, where the prices are "so cheap you
think you're robbing them"; the food is "delicate and
fine", but service is "excruciatingly slow" – "don't know if
I'm young enough to wait through another meal."*

Monroe's/M | 18 | 19 | 21 | $35 |
1968 Lombard St. (Webster St.), 567-4550
U – The Continental food served at this Lombard
Street spot "could be more exciting", but given its
"very romantic and intimate" setting, friendly service
and "quiet, classy" ambiance, it's a favorite for special
evenings anyway; besides, where else will you find
"great beef Wellington?"

Monsoon/LSM | – | – | – | E |
601 Van Ness Ave. (Turk St.), 441-3232
Slick and stylish Civic Center Chinese with food
designed by cookbook author Bruce Cost; some dishes
are dazzling, others are disappointing and service is
dunderheaded and often rude; prices are high for a city
full of good inexpensive Asian restaurants.

Mo's* | 20 | 14 | 17 | $15 |
1322 Grant Ave. (Green St.), 788-3779
U – "Delicious, juicy burgers" and great "homemade
fries" with real "homemade mayo" make this old-
fashioned North Beach spot a neighborhood favorite;
it's "noisy and busy all the time."

Nadine's/SM | 21 | 18 | 20 | $29 |
2400 San Pablo Ave. (Channing Way), Berkeley, 549-2807
U – "Off the beaten path but worth the trip", this
California-Continental is a "great secret" in the
Berkeley foodie world; its "interesting, everchanging
menu" offers "wonderful food" in a "cool, refreshing
atmosphere"; service is "personable and friendly."

Nan Yang/SM | 24 | 9 | 18 | $17 |
301 Eighth St. (Harrison St.), Oakland, 465-6924
M – One of the "best Burmese in the Bay Area" –
though "admittedly, there's not a lot of competition";
most praise this East Bay spot's "unique flavors" and
"cheap" prices, though some claim the food's "been
blanded out for the locals"; the decor is "simple and
casual" but "pleasing", and service attentive.

Narai/SM | 21 | 14 | 19 | $20 |
2229 Clement St. (24th Ave.), 751-6363
M – "Thai meets Chinese" at this "comfortable"
Richmond spot, yielding a "very interesting" and
appealing menu; "dishes look and taste wonderful"
and "the specials approach haute cuisine"; "very
reasonable prices" make it a "must-try."

San Francisco | F | D | S | C |

Narsai's Cafe/SM | 18 | 13 | 15 | $20 |

I. Magnin's basement, 135 Stockton St. (Geary Blvd.),
362-2100
*U – Quick, casual cafe in I. Magnin's basement which,
logically enough, is a convenient spot "to eat after
you've shopped 'til you've dropped"; soups, Caesar
salad, croissants and cappuccino are tops among the
limited offerings; critics chide owner Narsai to "get
serious and have a real menu."*

New Joe's/SM | 16 | 11 | 14 | $21 |

347 Geary Blvd. (Union Sq.), 989-6733
*U – Downtown Italian offering large portions of
"pedestrian Italian fare at inflated prices"; the "essence
of garlic prevails" here, and the atmosphere is "high-
tech but somehow cold"; service is a little ragged.*

New San Remo/SM | 16 | 19 | 16 | $24 |

2237 Mason St. (Chestnut St.), 673-9090
*M – "Not interesting enough but filling" neighborhood
Italian fare in North Beach (dinner only); some say
quality depends on the chef of the week – "the results
are either great or terrible"; still, this octogenarian is ok
"for a low-key evening", with a "nice, old-time
atmosphere" and "reasonable prices."*

Nicaragua Restaurant*/SM | 16 | 7 | 15 | $18 |

3015 Mission St. (Army St.), 826-3672
*M – "Big portions" of "authentic" Latin food in the
Mission; it's a "great deal" that "feels like you're in
Central America" and your wallet will hardly be dented
from this south-of-the-border excursion.*

Nob Hill Restaurant/SM | 21 | 18 | 20 | $39 |

Mark Hopkins Hotel, 1 Nob Hill (Mason St.), 391-9362
*M – Most surveyors think the French Nouvelle cuisine
served at this "small but quaint" Nob Hill spot is
"surprisingly good for a hotel restaurant", even though
it's pricey; adding to the favorable impression are
"beautiful flowers", a "relaxed ambiance" and
gracious service.*

Norman's Restaurant/SM | 18 | 18 | 17 | $29 |

3204 College Ave. (Alcatraz Ave.), Berkeley, 655-5291
*M – East Bay California cuisine restaurant that some
tout as having "great food and wine in a wonderful
atmosphere", while others decry as "pretentious and
disappointing"; though it can produce "zippy, interesting
flavors", this "upscale oasis" may prove unpredictable.*

North Beach Restaurant/LS | 17 | 14 | 16 | $27 |
1512 Stockton St. (bet. Green & Union Sts.), 392-1700
M – "Politicians, tourists and regulars" fill this family-
style Italian institution in North Beach; though critics
call the food "overpriced and unremarkable", a majority
calls it "hearty and consistent", with special praise
going to the "fresh pastas and fish" and homemade
prosciutto; service can be "indifferent" and the "tired"
decor needs "a face-lift"; upstairs seating is preferred.

North India Restaurant/SM | 21 | 16 | 18 | $24 |
3131 Webster Ave. (Lombard St.), 931-1556
U – This comfy Marina spot provides "possibly the best
Indian food in SF", with large portions of "authentic",
"incendiary" food; it has a "nice range of curries"and
"you can't go wrong" with choices from the tandoori
oven; service is efficient, but "be prepared to wait a bit,
even with reservations."

North Sea Village*/SM | 23 | 20 | 19 | $22 |
300 Turney St. (Bridgeway), Sausalito, 331-3300
U – Marin Chinese that gets high marks for its "dandy"
Hong Kong food, including "excellent dim sum" and
fresh seafood dishes; moderate prices, "comfortable"
setting and pleasant service make it an Asian treat.

Ocean City/SM | 19 | 13 | 13 | $14 |
640 Broadway (Columbus St.), 982-2328
M – Fans say this sprawling Chinatown place has "great
dim sum", "good, spicy seafood dishes" and decor that's
"ostentatious but just what a dim sum palace should
be"; critics call it "too big for comfort and too greasy"
to digest, but cheap prices keep it packed and pulsating.

Ocean Restaurant/SM | 22 | 8 | 13 | $16 |
726 Clement St. (8th Ave.), 221-3351
U – There's no atmosphere at this Richmond District
Cantonese, but you can't beat the price or the delicious
Chinese food; "when people ask for a good seafood
restaurant, send them here"; clay pot specials are
particularly good, but service can be brusque.

Old Swiss House/SM | 18 | 20 | 18 | $31 |
Pier 39 (Fisherman's Wharf), 434-0432
U – Believe it or not, there is decent food on tacky Pier
39; the Country Swiss food at this medium-priced spot
is of "home-cooked quality and the desserts are
magnificent"; it also boasts a "lovely view of the bay"
and a "warm" atmosphere; tourists have to eat, too.

Olivetto | 22 | 21 | 20 | $29 |
5655 College Ave. (Shafter Ave.), Oakland, 547-5356
*U – "Creativity abounds" at this lively East Bay
Mediterranean, which has a casual tapas and pizza cafe
downstairs and more serious fare upstairs; most call the
food "creative" and "tasty", with a "focus on organic
produce that's a big plus"; the setting is "very
comfortable" and attractive.*

Omnivore/SM | 18 | 14 | 20 | $26 |
3015 Shattuck Ave. (Emerson Ave.), Berkeley, 848-4346
*M – Reviewers are split on this East Bay Californian;
"sloppy cooking", "miscalculated and poorly
executed" say some, "perfectly prepared Continental
specialties" say others; in general, it's pleasant and
moderately priced with decent, albeit unreliable and
trendy, fare; has it slipped some with ownership change?*

1001 Nob Hill Restaurant/LSM | 18 | 24 | 18 | $46 |
1001 California St. (Mason St.), 441-1001
*U – Dazzling Nob Hill Continental that gets raves for
"magical" decor but more mixed reviews for the food,
ranging from "excellent" to just "ok"; most suggest,
however, current woes are just "growing pains" for this
important new restaurant; the bar/lounge is "very nice
when the music is good."*

Original Joe's/LSM | 18 | 11 | 17 | $19 |
144 Taylor St. (Turk St.), 775-4877
*M – "One of SF's fun old restaurants", this Italian
"throwback to the '40s" manages to survive in a "rotten
part" of the Tenderloin thanks to good burgers, roasts,
chops and other "great big heaps" of "traditional,
red-checked tablecloth food" at "reasonable prices";
critics call it "dull" and "boring", but its "predictability"
is part of its charm; "homey" is a nice way to describe
the decor; "watch your car – but enjoy the meal."*

Original Old Clam House/SM | 15 | 13 | 13 | $20 |
299 Bayshore Blvd. (Oakdale St.), 826-4880
*M – Though this Mission District seafood house still has
its fans ("I like it like an old friend"), a majority says it
has gone "downhill in the last decade" and become
"overpriced and overblown", especially after a recent
makeover; still, "some dishes are worthwhile"
("yummy" chowder, "marvelous" seafood specials)
and service is amiable; it's either "noisy and crowded"
or "dim and dismal", depending on when you go.*

Oritalia
| 22 | 18 | 19 | $27 |

1915 Fillmore St. (Bush St.), 346-1333
M – Do Asian and Italian food go together?; this attractive, appetizers-only Pacific Heights place thinks so; some say it's an "artificial mix that does not make it", others adore the "fascinating blend of flavors and textures" and the "great grazing"; warning: the "small plates can add up to big bucks" if you're hungry, but it's a "fun place to eat with a large party so everybody can sample and share."

Osome/SM
| 20 | 14 | 18 | $24 |

1923 Fillmore St. (Pine St.), 346-2311
M – Most say this Pacific Heights Japanese is still a good source for "top-notch" sushi, with "fresh, fresh" fish, simple decor and pleasant service; critics say it has "slipped in quality recently" and now serves "limp" sushi and other fare that "lacks excitement"; even so, it's a "fine neighborhood Japanese."

Osteria/M
| 22 | 17 | 19 | $26 |

3277 Sacramento St. (Presidio Ave.), 771-5030
See South of San Francisco Alphabetical Directory.

Pacific Cafe/SM
| 20 | 14 | 19 | $24 |

7000 Geary Blvd. (34th Ave.), 387-7091
Ghirardelli Sq., 900 North Point St. (Larkin St.), 775-1173
U – An oceanful of "fresh" fish is the specialty at these "unpretentious" seafood spots; "big portions", "great variety" and reasonable prices make them a "great value"; except for a no-reservations policy and consequent interminable waits, they're "easy to deal with for a decent meal."

Pacific Grill
| 22 | 23 | 22 | $41 |

(fka Portman Grill)
Pan Pacific Hotel, 500 Post St. (Mason St.), 771-8600
M – Reviewers agree that the decor is beautiful and "elegant" at this stylish Downtown hotel dining room; it's a "great spot for power breakfasts" but, as we went to press, the hotel ownership, restaurant name and chef changed; your guess is as good as ours.

PACIFIC HEIGHTS BAR & GRILL/SM
| 19 | 18 | 19 | $27 |

2001 Fillmore St. (Pine St.), 567-3337
U – Pacific Heights "yuppie heaven" social scene that's also "an oyster bar second to none"; the California wine list is fabulous as are most seafood and shellfish dishes, other foods are hit or miss; the place can be noisy, but the ambiance is attractive and "very comfortable" with breezy, friendly service; "a definitive SF scene."

Paloma/SM | 18 | 17 | 16 | $30 |

1585 University Ave. (Sacramento St.), Berkeley, 486-0132

M – The jury is still out on this expensive East Bay Tex-Mex that's under new management with a new emphasis on seafood; some are optimistic, calling it a "great revival", others say "new, but not improved."

Panama Hotel/S | 18 | 22 | 19 | $22 |

Panama Hotel, 4 Bay View St. (B St.), San Rafael, 457-3993

M – The charm of this "funky and eccentric" Marin restaurant lies in its garden setting ("like eating on the set of A Streetcar Named Desire") – it's especially nice on warm summer or fall evenings; the trendy Eclectic (Mexican to Thai cuisine, with everything in between) food is "surprisingly good sometimes", but "awful" on other occasions.

Paprika's Fono/SM | 17 | 19 | 18 | $25 |

Ghirardelli Sq., 900 North Point St. (bet. Polk & Larkin Sts.), 441-1223

M – "Touristy" but "lovely", this Hungarian standby in Ghirardelli Square also appeals to many locals; it's "hefty food, guaranteed to put on five pounds if you eat dessert"; favorites: langosh (fried bread) and hortobagi chicken; expect great views, moderate prices and "lots of tour buses."

PARK GRILL/SM | 23 | 24 | 22 | $33 |

Park Hyatt Hotel, 333 Battery St. (Clay St.), 296-2933

U – This dazzling, "truly elegant" California-Continental in a new Embarcadero Center hotel is "one of SF's best kept secrets", but not for long; it has "wonderful" food – including the "best hotel brunch in the city" – and "careful service"; a "great place to do business" over breakfast or lunch, it's relaxed and unhurried at dinner.

Parma/M | 23 | 16 | 23 | $24 |

3314 Steiner St. (Lombard St.), 567-0500

U – This moderately priced Italian is considered a "small Marina gem" thanks to "hearty food, lots of garlic and beyond-friendly service" ("you'll want to pinch the waiters"); don't miss "the best Caesar salad in SF"; the only problem: "where do you park?"

Pasha*/LSM | 14 | 20 | 17 | $29 |
1516 Broadway (Van Ness Ave.), 885-4477
*M – Slightly "seedy" Van Ness Middle Eastern that's
more popular for its show than its cooking – "too bad
the food isn't as good as the Arabic moccasins"; still, it's
"entertaining" and "exotic", and where else can you
see male and female belly dancers?*

Pasta Moon*/SM | 23 | 16 | 19 | $25 |
315 Main St. (Hwy. 92), Half Moon Bay, 726-5125
*U – "Delightful, out-of-the-way" little Italian find in Half
Moon Bay, offering "delicious food in a quaint and
cozy" setting; charming owners and helpful waiters also
win raves, prompting one enthusiastic surveyor to call it
the "best Italian outside of San Francisco."*

Perry's/LSM | 17 | 17 | 17 | $21 |
1944 Union St. (Laguna St.), 922-9022
*U – The ultimate San Francisco hangout with decent
food to boot; Perry Butler does all-American bar food
like none other; best bets: burgers, salads, sandwiches
and the calves liver; also good for Sunday brunch, it's
SF's "answer to P.J. Clarke's", so "put on an oxford,
khakis and penny loafers and say hi to Biff and Muffy."*

Phnom Penh/SM | – | – | – | M |
631 Larkin St. (Eddy St.), 775-5979
*This "excellent" Cambodian offers "exotic flavors at
affordable prices" in a "lousy" Tenderloin neighborhood,
but "move it to a better location and nobody would be
able to get in"; try the soups and curries and enjoy the
"happy" family atmosphere; on your way out, though,
"walk swiftly and have your car keys ready."*

PIERRE AT MERIDIEN/S | 23 | 23 | 23 | $45 |
Meridien Hotel, 50 Third St. (Market St.), 974-6400
*U – Enter this "ultra formal" haute cuisine temple and
"zap! you're in Paris, with soft music and a bill to match";
though the food is "excellent", the stratospheric prices
make some feel "it should be ten times better", and
sometimes "snooty" service causes one surveyor to
snort, "come now – who needs to be looked down on
at these prices?"; a new chef and remodeling job may
change the above rating.*

F	D	S	C

Pier 23 Cafe/S
| 16 | 16 | 15 | $21 |

Pier 23 (Embarcadero), 362-5125
M – On a sunny day, you can get a tan with your lunch
at this moderately priced, waterfront American; the
food ranges from "good" to "ok" and service is said to
be "unforgivable", but you can't beat the live jazz at
night or the sunny lunches and brunches on the pier;
try the meatloaf and the Chinese chicken salad.

Pietro's*/SM
| 18 | 23 | 17 | $23 |

1851 Union St. (Octavia St.), 563-4157
M – A "quaint" and "wonderfully romantic", grotto-like
setting gets top billing at this moderately priced Union
Street Italian; though some call it a "solid performer" in
the food department, others say it's just "ok if you need
Italian and other restaurants are booked"; both the
reception and service can be "cool."

Ping Yuen*/SMX
| 17 | 11 | 13 | $10 |

650 Jackson St. (Kearny St.), 986-6830
U – Incredibly cheap Chinese and American food in a
casual atmosphere in Chinatown; "low on service and
decor, but where else can you have a prime rib dinner
plus dessert and coffee for less than $10?"

Pixley Cafe/S
| 15 | 15 | 17 | $21 |

3127 Fillmore St. (bet. Filbert & Greenwich Sts.), 346-6123
M – Modern, clean Fillmore Street cafe serving "good,
basic" California-American fare – "great burgers" and
salads are the best items on the menu; it's "pleasant but
nothing to write home about" and "strangely
uncrowded."

Plearn Thai Cuisine/SMX
| 21 | 15 | 16 | $18 |

2050 University Ave. (Shattuck), Berkeley, 841-2148
M – "Thai one on" at this East Bay Asian, one of the
first Thai spots in the area and, many argue, still one of
"the best"; the food is "intensely flavorful" and
reasonably priced, and even critics who say it "used to
be better" admit it still has "some great dishes"; getting
a table here isn't easy – "bring sleeping bags and
prepare to wait."

Ploy Thai*
| 22 | 11 | 19 | $19 |

2232A Geary Blvd. (Divisadero St.), 563-8602
U – Small Pacific Heights spot with "pretty good Thai
food", "very friendly service" and a comfortable
setting; even if it's not much better than "average", low
prices make it worth a try.

| F | D | S | C |

POSTRIO/SM | 26 | 27 | 22 | $44 |
Prescott Hotel, 545 Post St. (Taylor St.), 776-7825
*U – Wolfgang Puck's prize-winning Downtown entry has
quickly become the Most Popular restaurant in town; fans
swoon over Annie and David Gingrass' "creative and
exciting" interpretations of California grill food, "perfect
pizzas" in the bar, and Pat Kuleto's jazzy and "seductive"
decor – a "knockout"; complaints include erratic, slow
service and "outrageous" waits for reservations; but the
combination of "quality and glitz" with that "wonderful
Wolfgang touch" equals "the best in SF."*

Prego Ristorante/LSM | 18 | 18 | 16 | $27 |
2000 Union St. (Buchanan St.), 563-3305
*M – "Trendy with a capital T" Union Street Italian
that's better for socializing than for dining; though some
praise the pizzas, pasta, chicken and focaccia, others
blast the food as "mass-produced" and served in
"ludicrously sparse" portions; but it's the stylish setting,
"lively atmosphere" and "party-scene" bar that are the
real draws here; if you must eat, opt for lunch when it's
less crowded and service is less harried.*

Regina's/LS | 21 | 23 | 20 | $34 |
Regis Hotel, 490 Geary Blvd. (Taylor St.), 928-7900
*U – Downtown spot featuring the authentic Cajun
cooking of chef Regina Charboneau; the food is "rich
but worth the calories", especially the eggplant
Lafayette, battered shrimp and jambalaya; an "elegant
setting and attentive service" help justify the high prices.*

Rice Table/SM | 21 | 15 | 19 | $22 |
1617 Fourth St., San Rafael, 456-1808
*M – "Bring an appetite" and enjoy large portions of
spicy Asian food at this "down-home" Marin Indonesian;
most pronounce it "authentic" and "good", not to
mention "relatively cheap"; all in all, it's worth a try for
a Far East change of pace.*

Riera's | 15 | 15 | 16 | $24 |
1539 Solano Ave. (Nielson St.), Berkeley, 527-1467
*M – One reviewer "left before eating because of the
rude service" at this East Bay Italian, and that may
have been a wise move in light of comments about the
food from those who stayed; moderate prices may be
its best attribute.*

Ristorante Fabrizio/SM | 20 | 15 | 21 |$26|
455 Magnolia Ave. (Ward St.), Larkspur, 924-3332
*M – Marin Italian trattoria that earns mixed notices; it's
a neighborhood favorite for some, thanks to its heavy
rich food, "family feeling" and "tightly packed" but
cozy setting; to others, it's merely "disappointing";
moderate prices make it easy to judge for yourself.*

Ristorante Grifone/LS | 17 | 17 | 17 |$27|
1609 Powell St. (Green St.), 397-8458
*M – North Beach Italian that inspires passionately
mixed responses; partisans praise "delicious veal" and
"best gnocchi in San Francisco"; detractors fume about
"terrible" service and "the worst" Italian food around;
only the decor gets good notices from all.*

Ristorante Milano | 24 | 15 | 21 |$25|
1448 Pacific Ave. (Hyde St.), 673-2961
*U – Some of "the best Italian food in SF" is served in
this tiny, simple trattoria at the back of Nob Hill; it's a
true neighborhood place with "wonderful homemade
pasta" and "polenta to die for", "personable" service
and a hostess that's "the best there is"; the only two
complaints, and they're serious ones, are that parking is
virtually impossible and the restaurant doesn't take
reservations; but overcoming those hurdles makes
dining here all the more satisfying.*

RODIN/M | 25 | 21 | 23 |$44|
1779 Lombard St. (bet. Laguna & Octavia), 563-8566
*U – Impressive Marina Nouvelle French that earns
enthusiastic praise from surveyors: "a poor man's
Masa's", "as good as Masa's and much less
expensive"; souffles are outstanding, particularly the
Grand Marnier, and though some find the atmosphere
a little too quiet and complain that portions are small,
most pronounce this romantic spot "a jewel."*

Ronayne's/SM | 12 | 13 | 16 |$24|
1799 Lombard St. (Laguna St.), 922-5060
*M – Most say go elsewhere to catch a seafood meal;
this moderately priced Marina spot is "not very good",
though some find it a serviceable, unpretentious
alternative to the big, commercial (i.e., Fisherman's
Wharf) fish places.*

F	D	S	C

Roosevelt Tamale Parlor/SMX | 17 | 7 | 12 | $11 |

2817 24th St. (Bryant St.), 550-9213

U – "Don't miss this dive if you love Mexican food"; in the heart of the Mission, it offers good, cheap eats, with chicken chimichangas, tamales and deluxe chicken tostadas recommended; despite mostly enthusiastic comments, food ratings have slipped significantly from last year, generating a few zingers like "there has to be better places – and there are"; Christmas lights add to the kitschy, but fun, ambiance.

Roti/SM | 21 | 21 | 19 | $33 |

Hotel Griffon, 155 Steuart St. (bet. Mission & Howard Sts.), 495-2100

M – Pricey, new Downtown American-Country French creation by Cindy Pawlcyn (Fog City Diner, Bix, Mustard's); while most agree the "rotisserie chicken is to die for", as are the french fries and onion rings, the rest of the menu gets wildly mixed reviews: "Cindy scores again" vs. "hard to believe Cindy P. is behind this mess"; "shockingly mediocre" vs. "the best in town"; the dining room can be noisy and service can be "snotty, snitty, snooty"; only time will tell.

Rotunda, The | 17 | 23 | 18 | $26 |

Neiman-Marcus, 150 Stockton St. (Geary Blvd.), 362-4777

U – Why shop 'til you drop when you can fortify yourself at this elegant Downtown department store; the food is merely "reliable", and pricey at that, but ladies who lunch like the popovers, lobster salad and Bloody Marys, charming service and a great view of Union Square; a good place to satisfy voyeuristic impulses: "don't forget your white gloves"; "a great place to take Granny for tea."

Royal Thai/S | 23 | 15 | 19 | $19 |

610 Third St. (Irwin St.), San Rafael, 485-1074
951 Clement St. (11th St.), 386-1795

U – Terrific Marin Thai (now with a new branch in San Francisco) that serves some of the "best Thai food around" – moderately priced seafood dishes are especially delicious and very unusual; incongruously located in a Victorian house under the freeway, it has a charming, exotic atmosphere complete with huge photos of Thailand's king and queen.

San Francisco

| **F** | **D** | **S** | **C** |

Ruby's/SM

| – | – | – | M |

489 Third St. (Bryant St.), 541-0795
*With excellent sandwiches, pizzas and pastas, this
wood-lined SOMA trattoria may be a little pricey for
finger food, but its charming, friendly service packs
them in at lunch; the new Downtown business crowd
has made it a "hot spot."*

Rue de Main*

| 23 | 21 | 20 | $30 |

22622 Main St. (bet. B & C Aves.), Hayward, 537-0812
*M – Moderately priced French restaurant in Hayward
that wins mostly praise for its "hearty but delicate"
old-world food and attractive mural decor; though
some say both the food and atmosphere are "dark and
musty", most call it "a point of light in the provinces"
and "one of the nicer spots in this culinary wilderness."*

Sally's/SMX

| 19 | 12 | 13 | $12 |

300 De Haro (16th St.), 626-6006
*U – Inexpensive Potrero Hill spot that wins raves as the
"best place for muffins and cinnamon rolls in the Bay
Area"; with its "all-American" food and decor, it's great
for breakfast or cafeteria-style lunch; but come early
because this charming spot has caught on and there
can be a wait.*

Sam's Anchor Cafe/SM

| 12 | 20 | 13 | $21 |

27 Main St. (Tiburon Blvd.), Tiburon, 435-4527
*U – This moderately priced Marin seafood cafe has
"bimbo service and food to match, but no one goes
here for either one"; the real idea is to "sit out on the
sunny deck, watch the sailboats come in", "work on
your tan and enjoy a beer"; but if you must eat, stick to
burgers; go early on sunny weekends – the wait can be
extraordinary.*

Sam's Grill & Seafood/M

| 21 | 15 | 17 | $26 |

374 Bush St. (Kearny St.), 421-0594
*U – A San Francisco classic, this moderately priced
Downtown grill offers great seafood, elegant decor and
a "really old-time" atmosphere, making it a top choice
for business lunches; sand dabs, porterhouse and veal
loin chops are especially recommended; some prefer
relaxed dinners over the noontime hustle-bustle, when
service is apt to be at its "rude and crusty" best.*

| F | D | S | C |

Samui*/M
| 24 | 16 | 24 | $17 |

2414 Lombard St. (Scott St.), 563-4405

U – A Thai winner, this charming Marina Asian offers "Samui [Southern Thai] Island cuisine [that's] uniquely spiced", "well-conceived" and "balanced"; the food is "unusual, good and inexpensive" with curried duck and seafood among the highlights; a cozy setting and attentive service from the owner and his family add appeal.

Samurai*/SM
| 21 | 17 | 18 | $23 |

2633 Bridgeway St., Sausalito, 332-8245

M – Some say this moderately priced Marin sushi spot is "quite good", others say it's "not the freshest"; but it's certainly "ok if you're in the neighborhood", even though decor and service could use some work.

San Francisco BBQ/S
| 20 | 10 | 18 | $13 |

1328 18th St. (bet. Missouri & Texas Sts.), 431-8956

U – Thai barbecue spot on Potrero Hill that "can't be beat for taste and price"; "noodle and salad combos are good", as are the barbecued chicken salad and ribs; if short on atmosphere, with this much taste at so little cost, who cares?; "a jewel for takeout."

Sanppo/SMX
| 19 | 13 | 15 | $18 |

1702 Post St. (Buchanan St.), 346-3486

M – Opinion is split on this recently redecorated, old-time Japantown spot; some say the relatively inexpensive fare is "the best Japanese in SF", others find "quality is slipping"; it can get crowded and "service can be agonizingly slow."

Santa Fe Bar & Grill/LSM
| 18 | 18 | 16 | $30 |

1310 University Ave. (bet. Sacramento & San Pueblo Sts.), Berkeley, 841-4740

M – Once Jeremiah Tower's home base, this pricey East Bay Southwestern, located in a former Berkeley railroad station, is now just a "faded cactus flower" to critics, who blast "bad food", noise and service lapses – "we thought our waiter had resigned halfway through our meal"; optimists, however, insist that it's "on the comeback trail", and recommend the ceviche, black bean soup, grilled meats and martinis.

S. Asimakopoulous/SM
| 18 | 12 | 16 | $19 |

288 Connecticut St. (18th St.), 552-8789

U – Inexpensive Potrero Hill neighborhood place that some say offers the "best Greek food in town" in an authentic taverna setting; try the hot appetizer plate and "terrific lamb"; the decor is "tacky" with friendly, but bumbling, service.

Saul's Delicatessen/SMX | 17 | 11 | 15 | $16 |

1475 Shattuck Ave. (Vine St.), Berkeley, 848-3354
U – If you want real deli food, you'd better go to New
York, but this mid-priced Berkeley spot is an ok
substitute for those without plane tickets – "not a NY deli,
not even LA, but good"; latkes and pastrami sandwiches
are satisfying, but "will someone please tell me why the
Bay Area and good delis are a contradiction in terms?"

Savannah Grill/SM | 19 | 19 | 19 | $27 |

55 Tamal Vista Blvd. (Madera Rd.), Corte Madera,
924-6774
M – Noisy, yupped-out California cuisine eatery with a
wildly eclectic menu that has its ups and downs –
"some dishes outstanding, some barely standing"; still,
fans love the numerous choices and creativity at this
newly remodeled Marin spot – not to mention the
"great bar scene."

Savoy Brasserie/SM | – | – | – | E |

580 Geary Blvd. (Jones St.), 441-2700
As we go to press, this swanky French bistro has just
opened; a welcome addition to SF's Downtown scene,
it has white tiles, dark wood and brass, a stylish bar and
great oyster selection; it's a sophisticated supper club
that has immediately become popular with the carriage
trade despite being expensive.

Schroeder's/M | 16 | 17 | 17 | $23 |

240 Front St. (bet. California & Sacramento), 421-4778
M – Reviewers hope a recent ownership change will
liven up the "tired" German fare at this moderately
priced Downtown classic; "both food and service could
be lots better", but some still love the "good, hearty food"
and insist the sauerkraut and bratwurst can't be beat.

Scoma's/S | 17 | 16 | 15 | $27 |

Pier 47 (Jefferson St.), 771-4383
588 Bridgeway, Sausalito, 332-9551,
M – Though these moderately priced waterfront spots
are popular with out-of-towners, most locals rate the
seafood anywhere from "mediocre" to "awful": "heavy
on oily sauces", "leave it for the tourists"; fans,
however, call the Jefferson Street branch "one of the
better Fisherman's Wharf" spots, and advise "never
leave San Francisco without their cioppino"; service
can be brusque, but great Bay views compensate.

Scott's Seafood Grill and Bar/SM | 18 | 17 | 17 | $26 |
2400 Lombard St. (Scott St.), 563-8988
3 Embarcadero Ctr. (Sacramento & Drum Sts.), 981-0622
*M – Not bad for a moderately priced seafood chain, but
then "not your best choice" for fish, either; though they
offer "some good dishes", others "taste like styrofoam"
and are "not always fresh"; the Lombard Street
location gets the highest ratings.*

Sears Fine Foods/SMX | 19 | 10 | 17 | $14 |
439 Powell St. (bet. Post & Sutter Sts.), 986-1160
*M – "We'd pay many silver dollars for their pancakes",
say fans of this Union Square breakfast/lunch institution;
it's great for simple dishes like pancakes, corned beef
hash, waffles and the like, but "keep away from most
everything else"; sassy waitresses add to the diner
ambiance and help make it a great place to take the
kids for a Downtown expedition; no dinner.*

Sedona Grill and Bar/SM | 24 | 23 | 21 | $33 |
Shattuck Hotel, 2086 Allston Way (Shattuck Ave.),
Berkeley, 841-3848
*U – This East Bay Southwestern "looks great, tastes good
and costs lots", but most feel it's well worth it for
"wonderful flavors and always top ingredients" that
"prove that taste need not be sacrificed when being
inventive"; service and the "desert" setting also win raves.*

Seoul Garden*/LS | 21 | 17 | 17 | $20 |
Japantown, 22 Peace Plaza (bet. Laguna & Webster Sts.),
563-7664
*U – For a fun and delicious change of pace, head for
this moderately priced Korean in Japantown; it has the
"best Korean BBQ" in town – cooked tableside on
traditional grills – along with other spicy, unusual fare, a
modest but attractive setting and attentive service from
kimonoed waitresses; kids especially love this place.*

Shadows, The/S | 13 | 20 | 14 | $37 |
1349 Montgomery St. (Union St.), 982-5536
*U – The view is great but the food isn't at this expensive
Telegraph Hill French – "wish we'd brought a picnic",
"only for tourists"; most find the setting "romantic", but
nothing else about the place lives up to it.*

Siam Cuisine/LSM | 20 | 14 | 17 | $19 |
1181 University Ave. (San Pablo Ave.), Berkeley, 548-3278
*M – Bangkok natives say this delicious Berkeley Thai
"tastes like home"; spicy red snapper and peanut
noodles are favorites among the authentic, fire-eater fare;
"pleasant surroundings", efficient service and moderate
prices add to the appeal; critics insist it "was once great,
now remodeled and a shadow of its former self."*

Silks/S | 20 | 25 | 21 | $43 |
Mandarin Oriental Hotel, 222 Sansome St. (California St.),
986-2020
*M – Most reviewers agree that the expensive Nouvelle
cuisine served at this opulent hotel dining room has
slipped since chef Howard Bulka left, leaving the place
"lovely but lackluster"; still, some enjoy its "elegant
presentation of good food" and no one denies the
wonderful ambiance of the quiet, attractive dining
room; service is skillful but slow.*

690 | 19 | 18 | 17 | $30 |
690 Van Ness Ave. (Turk St.), 255-6900
*M – Whacked-out Caribbean with decor to match is
what to expect at Jeremiah Tower's new Civic Center
place around the corner from his Stars; some
reviewers love the "zesty food" and "strange, but
good, combinations"; perhaps as a result of too high
expectations, other reviewers find the expensive fare
"self-conscious, pretentious" and simply "lousy"; it's
big, it's noisy, it's a real scene.*

South China Cafe/S | – | – | – | I |
4133 18th St. (Castro St.), 861-9323
*Despite no decor, this Castro Cantonese hole-in-the-wall
cafe is popular with some for its decent food (especially
pot stickers and wonton soup) and good service;
others, however, find it "too funky" and recommend
staying home.*

South Park Cafe | 20 | 18 | 18 | $25 |
108 South Park Ave. (bet. 2nd & 3rd Sts.), 495-7275
*U – If you can't fly to Paris, drive to this moderately
priced bistro on a sunny SOMA street for much the
same effect; "merveilleux" – "a sleeper", "hate to share
how good it is for the price", "the mussels are always
like butter and there's a wonderful sweetbread salad";
most find the ambiance "intimate and comfy"; if it's
crowded with "tables on top of each other", "c'est Paris."*

Spenger's Fish Grotto/LSM | 11 | 10 | 11 | $21 |

1919 Fourth St. (University Ave.), Berkeley, 845-7771

U – This huge East Bay seafood spot owes its existence
mostly to cheap drinks and the nearby UC campus; our
surveyors suggest the fish is only edible if you've had
six or seven drinks, which might also help you overlook
the "slam-bam service and ambiance."

Spiedini/S | 20 | 19 | 18 | $29 |

101 Ygnacio Valley Rd. (Oakland Blvd.), Walnut Creek,
939-2100

M – Trendy East Bay Italian with "good food"; it's "very
accommodating to children" and, as a result, is often
very noisy and some say it becomes a "large day-care
center"; check out the grilled meats and pizzas.

Splendido's/SM | 20 | 22 | 18 | $30 |

4 Embarcadero (bet. Drumm & Clay Sts.), 986-3222

U – Moderately expensive Downtown Italian trend-
orama with "great" pizza, grazing and "divine
desserts" that cause fans to say "they're doing
something right"; popular from its opening, "on the
trend scale it's hot, hot, hot"; the Pat Kuleto decor is
"cool", i.e., "spectacular, if a bit LA-ish."

Spuntino/LSM | 18 | 16 | 13 | $16 |

524 Van Ness Ave. (McAllister St.), 861-7772

U – Perfect for a quick bite before the opera or
symphony, this moderately priced, Civic Center
"no-frills" Italian offers "wonderful Italian fast food",
including pizza and plump foccacia sandwiches; coffee
and desserts also make this worth a stop.

SQUARE ONE/SM | 24 | 19 | 21 | $38 |

190 Pacific Ave. (Front St.), 788-1110

U – This Mediterranean-International spot draws raves
for its top-notch, everchanging menu, prepared under
the caring stewardship of star chef-owner Joyce
Goldstein; "no restaurant matches the power and range
of cooking here", with homemade breads and pastas
singled out for special kudos; "unobtrusive" service is a
plus, somewhat "sterile" decor a minus; critics say both
its prices and reputation are too high; a very active
wine program under the direction of Joyce's son, Evan,
is a plus.

| **F** | **D** | **S** | **C** |

Squid's Cafe/M
| 14 | 13 | 14 | $20 |

96 McAllister St. (Leavenworth St.), 861-0100
*M – Though tentacle lovers still enjoy the dozen ways
they do squid at this Tenderloin seafood spot, a
majority carps that food quality has sunk and says it
"should be docked" for "lack of taste"; still, moderate
prices, a funky black-and-pink setting and free-flowing
Anchor Steam on tap help keep this "late-night retro
hangout" afloat.*

Squire Restaurant & Wine Cellar, The/SM
| 21 | 24 | 23 | $47 |

Fairmont Hotel, 950 Mason St. (California St.), 772-5211
*U – Fancy, expensive and, most say, worth it, this
Continental hotel dining room specializes in traditional
seafood and quality meats; reviewers praise the
"beautiful room, great cuisine" and "best service" –
"everything was great, especially the lamb saddle and
garnishes"; some find it too stuffy and warn "keep
away if you're under 40" – or on a budget.*

Stanford Park/S
| 16 | 17 | 15 | $30 |

Stanford Park Hotel, 100 El Camino Real, Menlo Park,
322-1234
*U – Given its "ordinary" hotel food, "untrained,
unwilling personnel" and high prices, it's no wonder
this Peninsula American draws brickbats: "not much
atmosphere", "instant cappuccino – ugh!", "avoid like
the plague"; numerous chef changes notwithstanding,
ratings are at least respectable.*

STARS/LSM
| 25 | 22 | 21 | $41 |

150 Redwood Alley (bet. McAllister & Golden Gate Aves.),
861-7827
*U – Jeremiah Tower's bustling, brassy Civic Center
area brasserie is lunchtime home to San Francisco's
"see-and-be-seen" glitterati; nearly everyone finds
Stars' American food "wonderful and creative" with
grilled salmon, lamb shanks and desserts getting special
raves; it's "a tough place to get into, but well worth the
persistence"; whether you consider it noisy or lively,
friendly or rushed depends on your point of view; but if
you haven't been there, you should find out for yourself.*

Stars Cafe | 22 | 15 | 18 | $23 |
555 Golden Gate Ave. (bet. Van Ness & Polk Aves.),
861-4344
*U – A "casual version of Stars", this moderately priced
California cafe serves small portions of its big sister's
food at much lower prices, making it a "good bargain";
Caesar salad, fish and chips, and fish sandwiches are
among our surveyors' favorites, but critics say the food
doesn't shine as much as Stars' and complain of
"inattentive service."*

Straits Cafe/S | 17 | 13 | 16 | $18 |
3300 Geary Blvd. (Parker St.), 668-1783
*M – If you like it spicy, you'll love this inexpensive,
Singapore-style cafe in the Richmond District; if not,
order carefully; fire-eaters praise the "excellent and
unusual" fare – especially the "wonderful appetizers
and chicken dishes" – and brand it "probably the best
bargain in town."*

SWAN OYSTER DEPOT/MX | 24 | 13 | 21 | $18 |
1517 Polk St. (bet. California & Sacramento), 673-1101
*U – "Landmark" seafood luncheonette that's truly a
classic San Francisco experience; whether you take it
out or eat in, you can't beat the fresh seafood, oysters
or what may be the feel-good dish of the century, clam
chowder; with straw on the floor and rickety stools at
the counter, it has "no decor, but a wonderful '30s
atmosphere"; add "friendly service" and moderate prices
and you'll agree, "it doesn't get any better than this."*

TADICH GRILL/M | 21 | 18 | 17 | $27 |
240 California St. (Battery St.), 391-2373
*U – "Fresh fish makes up for rude service any day" at
this Downtown seafood stalwart, known for its long
waits, antique ambiance and "good American food"
done "the old-fashioned way, thank goodness" (try the
petrale sole, sand dabs, fries and rice pudding); though
some say it used to be better, try telling that to the "old
boy" crowd of bankers and lawyers who keep the place
perpetually packed.*

Taiwan Restaurant/LSM | 16 | 12 | 12 | $14 |
2071 University Ave. (Shattuck Ave.), Berkeley, 845-1456
*M – This inexpensive East Bay Chinese can be
delicious or horrible, depending on what you order;
while it has "some outstanding dishes", others
resemble "Chinese food as it would be prepared by
your high school cafeteria"; lemon chicken is a safe bet.*

San Francisco

| F | D | S | C |

Tanuki/SM

| – | – | – | M |

4419 California St. (6th Ave.), 752-5740
A real "sleeper", this friendly, comfortable and inexpensive Richmond Japanese has a "good sushi bar", "fine cold noodle salad and teriyaki dishes", and other "plain good Japanese food"; regulars are treated especially well – the sushi chef may even surprise them with "little treats on the side."

Taqueria Mission/LSMX

| 20 | 7 | 11 | $10 |

4798 Mission (28th St.), 469-5053
M – Some say this hole-in-the-wall Mission District Mexican offers the "best burrito in the world", along with other wonderful and "consistent" south-of-the-border favorites; others call it "nothing special" – but at these low prices, why quibble?; great for takeout, too; P.S. try the cantaloupe drink.

Tarantino's Restaurant/SM

| 12 | 14 | 15 | $29 |

206 Jefferson St. (Taylor St.), 775-5600
M – A seafood strikeout at Fisherman's Wharf; reviewers marvel that this expensive piece of "wharf junk" is still open; though some say the seafood here is "ok" for the area, most call it a "tourist trap" that is most adept at reeling in wallets.

THEP PHANOM/SM

| 26 | 16 | 20 | $20 |

400 Waller St. (Fillmore St.), 431-2526
U – The Survey's highest rated Asian for the second year in a row and the "best Thai in the city", this moderately priced lower Haight restaurant is a scrumptious taste treat, thanks to "complex flavors" and "the most exquisite sauces" around; pleasant service and decor add to the enjoyment; not surprisingly, it's popular and often has lines.

Thornhill Cafe/S

| 22 | 19 | 20 | $27 |

5761 Thornhill Dr. (Grisborne St.), Oakland, 339-0646
U – Reviewers love the charming atmosphere and wonderfully Eclectic food at this moderately priced East Bay restaurant; "what a gem" – it's like a bit of country in the middle of the city; Sunday brunch in the "lovely backyard" is a favorite; hospitable owners and attentive service also win applause.

| | **F** | **D** | **S** | **C** |

Ti Bacio/SM
| | 19 | 14 | 19 | $23 |

5301 College Ave. (Broadway), Oakland, 428-1703
U – "A place to indulge without the guilt", this East Bay
Italian is "fighting the low cholesterol fight and turning
out some pretty good meals in the process"; try the
garlic bread, linguine with clam sauce and other
good-tasting, good-for-you fare; it's small and, not
surprisingly, usually crowded.

Tien Fu/SM
| | 15 | 10 | 13 | $15 |

1395 Noriega St. (21st Ave.), 665-1064
U – Though some say this Noe Valley Szechuan still
turns out reasonably good food (try the green onion
cakes) at fair prices, a majority feels it's "slipping" and
is now most useful for takeout, especially in view of the
grungy decor and "rude service" – "if you ask for a
fork, the waiter is likely to throw one at you."

Tommaso's/SM
| | 22 | 15 | 17 | $20 |

1042 Kearny St. (Broadway), 398-9696
U – Majority choice for the "best pizza in SF";
reviewers rave about the "yummy" pies that come out
of this North Beach establishment's wood-burning
oven; funky atmosphere, tough waitresses and small,
noisy, crowded quarters are part of the package, as are
long waits at peak hours.

Tommy's Joynt/LSMX
| | 13 | 13 | 10 | $13 |

1101 Geary Blvd. (Van Ness Ave.), 775-4216
U – Raffish cafeteria-hofbrau near Van Ness that some
call a "mysterious San Francisco tradition" – where
else can you get authentic buffalo stew (even if it's not
very good), a variety of sandwiches and over a
hundred beers to wash it all down with?; though critics
label it "a dump", one fan says, "when I want the
greasiest roast beef sandwich, this is the place"; with
trinkets and junk covering every inch, the atmosphere
is definitely funky.

Tommy Toy's Chinoise/SM
| | 23 | 26 | 23 | $40 |

655 Montgomery St. (bet. Washington & Clay), 397-4888
U – Chic Downtown Chinese that wins raves on every
count: "absolutely inspired cooking", "very helpful
help", "unlike any Chinese you've ever experienced –
totally elegant"; for the best experience, avoid the prix
fixe meals and "insist on ordering from the menu –
though you may have to arm wrestle the waiter to do
this"; prices are high and some feel portions are way
too small, but most say it's "worth every cent."

San Francisco | F | D | S | C |

Ton Kiang/SM | 20 | 8 | 14 | $16 |

3148 Geary Blvd. (Spruce St.), 752-4440
5827 Geary Blvd. (22nd Ave.) , 387-8273
*U – Delicious Hakka (Northern Chinese) dishes and
low prices make up for the lack of atmosphere at this
Richmond District duo whose diners "crave their
chicken in wine sauce"; other recommended dishes
include black bean crab, salt and pepper squid and red
and green dipping sauces; for best results, take your
waiter's advice.*

Tortola Restaurant/S | 18 | 16 | 17 | $21 |

3640 Sacramento St. (Spruce St.), 929-8181
*M – Some love and some hate the California-Mexican
food at this Pacific Heights spot; battered and
cheese-stuffed chili is "one of the best Mexican-inspired
dishes in the city", but other offbeat dishes don't always
work; still, the majority applauds its efforts.*

Tourelle/SM | 19 | 24 | 19 | $35 |

3565 Mt. Diablo Blvd. (Oak Hui Rd.), Lafayette, 284-3565
*M – This East Bay French gets raves for its pretty
"atrium-like setting and jazz on weekends", but mixed
reviews for its expensive food; it does have "some great
dishes" and, on the right night, can be a "rare find";
too often, however, this is a case of "so close yet so far."*

TRADER VIC'S/LSM | 15 | 20 | 19 | $38 |

20 Cosmo Place (Taylor St.), 776-2232
9 Anchor Dr. (Powell St.), Emeryville, 653-3400
*M – This Downtown institution is going through a
gradual facelift, but keeping its basic Kon-Tiki style; it
does a brisk trade with tourists and is a "favorite for a
big evening" for some locals; if you eat here, sauteed
seafood and Chinese barbecued meats are best bets;
children find the decor amusing, and the Captain's
Club is an "in" ladies' lunch spot; a new chef Alfred
Schilling has not been around long enough to make a
major impact on food ratings.*

Trattoria Contadina/LSM | 18 | 15 | 17 | $24 |

1800 Mason St. (Union St.), 982-5728
*U – This tiny Russian Hill trattoria may not serve the
best food around, but it is "hearty and satisfying", as
well as moderately priced; with its caring service and
casual atmosphere, it's become something of a hangout
for local celebrities – "look for the stars, they know
what to eat"; reservations are a must here.*

Trio Cafe/SX | 20 | 17 | 20 | $13 |

1870 Fillmore St. (bet. Bush & Sutter Sts.), 563-2248
*U – Good salads and sandwiches and huge cups of cafe
au lait help make this little Pacific Heights breakfast/
lunch spot a big favorite with locals; linger at a table or
grab a quick bite at the counter – either way, you'll
enjoy good vibes.*

Triple Rock Brewery/LSMX | 14 | 14 | 11 | $12 |

1920 Shattuck Ave. (University Ave.), Berkeley, 843-2739
*U – "There's no such thing as one drink at the Triple
Rock" where "great brew", made on the premises,
draws a lively, noisy young crowd; chili, nachos and
sandwiches are ok and cheap but drinking, not eating,
is the main attraction here; for best results, bring a
bunch of friends and sample the variety of suds – but
leave the car keys at home.*

Tu Lan* | 23 | 3 | 12 | $12 |

8 Sixth St. (Market St.), 626-0927
*U – "Don't let the decor or location fool you" – though
both are abysmal, the food at this inexpensive
Vietnamese in the Tenderloin is "wonderful" and
"worth stepping over the winos for"; don't miss the
delicious imperial rolls; no reserving may mean a wait.*

Tung Fong/S | 23 | 8 | 13 | $13 |

808 Pacific Ave. (Stockton St.), 362-7115
*U – Some of the most delicious dim sum in the city can
be found at this cheap and funky Chinatown hole-in-the-
wall; "best steamed pork buns in the Bay Area, and
I've eaten a lot" is a typical comment; they're not big
on service or decor "but that helps keep the tourists away."*

Tutto Bene/LSM | 18 | 19 | 17 | $29 |

2080 Van Ness Ave. (Pacific Ave.), 673-3500
*M – "Go for the bar scene and skip the overpriced
food" at this glitzy Van Ness trattoria; though some
praise the antipasti and pastas, most say the rest of the
menu is "more fluff than substance"; decent service
and good-looking decor are pluses.*

231 Ellsworth/M | 24 | 21 | 23 | $40 |

231 N. Ellsworth Ave. (bet. 2nd & 3rd Aves.), San Mateo,
347-7231
*M – "At last the Peninsula has a restaurant as good as
any in the city", cheer fans of this "superb and elegant"
French; with its "innovative" cuisine, "savvy wine list"
and "attractive" decor, it's a "visual and olefactory
pleasure" and "a rare find" in the suburbs; a few
dissenters contend it's "good but not spectacular",
"pretentious and overpriced."*

Umberto's/SM | 17 | 20 | 17 | $29 |
141 Steuart St. (bet. Mission & Howard Sts.), 543-8021
*M – Subterranean SOMA Northern Italian that "used
to be good", but is now "in a rut" with "blah" food
that "needs some pep"; still, the pasta can be "great"
and some find the "cool and dark" basement setting
pleasantly reminiscent of a wine cellar; it's a "good,
out-of-the-way place" for a business lunch, even
though service can be "slo-o-o-w."*

Uncle Yu's*/SM | 10 | 11 | 13 | $25 |
999 Oak Hill Rd. (Mt. Diablo Blvd.), Lafayette, 283-1688
2005 Crow Canyon Pl., San Ramon, 275-1818
*M – "Untypical Chinese strip mall-type restaurant" with
food that qualifies as "great Chinese for Contra Costa",
but not so great anywhere else – "very pedestrian",
"nothing exciting", "surrendering to the suburban
palate"; at least it's "good for kids."*

Undici/M | – | – | – | M |
374 Eleventh St. (Harrison St.), 431-3337
*This hip Southern Italian in the former Taxi location is
one of the new "hot spots"; smack in the heart of the
SOMA bustle, the draw here is the street traffic and the
scene; the trendy angel hair pastas and little pizzas are
good, but nothing to rave home to Mama about.*

U.S. Restaurant/SMX | 15 | 10 | 17 | $14 |
431 Columbus Ave. (bet. Green & Stockton), 362-6251
*U – "The place to go if you like lots to eat, cheap", this
"basic, no-frills" North Beach Southern Italian provides
"hefty" portions of "homey", "honestly prepared"
food with "no pretensions"; "vegetables never heard of
al dente" here, but the "meatball sandwiches are worth
it alone"; it may be "plain and ugly", but it's a
"tradition" and a "square deal for a square meal."*

Vanessi's/LSM | 17 | 16 | 17 | $30 |
1177 California St. (Jones St.), 771-2422
*M – Surveyors debate whether the move from North
Beach to Nob Hill has helped or hurt this old-line
Italian; fans say it's "still home away from home to the
regulars", thanks to its "good solid food" and "nice
atmosphere"; critics say it's "stale and old fogeyish",
"riding on its reputation."*

| F | D | S | C |

Vegi Food*/SMX | 19 | 9 | 15 |$13|
1820 Clement St. (bet. 19th & 20th Aves.), 387-8111
*M – Relive "1960s Berkeley" at this Asian Vegetarian
cafe in the Richmond District; try the delicious
deep-fried walnuts, "best hot and sour soup in town"
and other bargain-priced veggie fare; along with no
meat, beer, wine or MSG, it also has no decor, so the
best strategy may be to "order the walnuts to go."*

Viareggio/S | 18 | 18 | 20 |$26|
1956½ Lombard St. (bet. Webster & Buchanan Sts.),
921-1812
*M – Though some say that "quality has declined with
new ownership", you can still enjoy a "delicious" meal
at this Lombard Street Italian "if you know what to
order"; most people apparently don't, however, since
the place is "never crowded"; a good wine list, "pretty"
setting and "friendly" service are pluses.*

Via Veneto/SM | 14 | 12 | 16 |$19|
5356 College Ave. (Broadway), Oakland, 652-8540
*M – "Your basic, dusty plastic grapes kind of old-line
place", this East Bay Southern Italian serves
"standard" red-sauce fare that's "satisfactory", if
"nothing sensational"; fans call it a "pleasant place"
that's "great for kids."*

Vicolo Pizzeria/SMX | 22 | 11 | 11 |$14|
201 Ivy St. (bet. Franklin & Gough Sts.), 863-2382
Ghirardelli Sq., 900 North Point St. (bet. Larkin & Polk
Sts.), 776-1331
*U – Most rave about the cornmeal crusts and designer
toppings at this wharf pizzeria: "best pizza west of the
Hudson", "unique", "fabulous"; even those who scorn
nouvelle-style pies admit, "it ain't pizza but I still like it."*

Victor's/SM | 22 | 26 | 23 |$48|
St. Francis Hotel, 335 Powell St. (Geary Blvd.), 956-7777
*M – "Tres elegante" French perched atop the St.
Francis Hotel that offers a "fabulous" view, "lovely"
setting, "wonderful" service and "great wine list"; those
attributes make it easier to forgive the sometimes
"so-so" food and high prices; given the setting, it's
"great for Sunday brunch" and "hard to beat for a
special occasion."*

Vivande Porta Via/SM | 24 | 17 | 18 | $22 |

2125 Fillmore St. (bet. California & Sacramento Sts.),
346-4430

U – *"If only they served dinner", sigh fans of Carlo Middone's "sparkling" Pacific Heights deli/trattoria; as it is, fans gladly jam into this lunch-only spot for "great pastas and salads", "terrific sausage" and other "delightful Sicilian fare"; those put off by long lines, crowded conditions and "erratic" service in the rear cafe can opt for takeout from the front deli counter; either way, it's pricey but "worth it."*

Vlasta's European*/S | 19 | 12 | 19 | $23 |

2420 Lombard St. (Scott St.), 931-7533

U – *A "wonderful break from designer food", this old-fashioned Marina Hungarian provides "terrific" duck, "wonderful" bread dumplings and other "heavy", "hearty" Central European fare; "every neighborhood should have one" – just don't try to stay awake after dinner.*

WASHINGTON SQUARE | 17 | 17 | 17 | $27 |
BAR & GRILL/LSM

1707 Powell St. (Union St.), 982-8123

U – *"More a club than a restaurant", the "Washbag", as this North Beach "institution" is known, is the place where local celebs and media types gather to "hear the latest gossip and drown in martinis"; the quasi-Italian food is downright "average", but basics like meatloaf and Joe's special are reliably good, and you "don't come here to eat", anyway; "nice piano jazz", "great energy" and "fun, friendly people" are three more reasons it's a favorite "see-and-be-seen" hangout.*

Waterfront Restaurant/SM | 18 | 22 | 17 | $28 |

Pier 7, Embarcadero (Broadway), 391-2696

U – *The fish is "always fresh" and the views always "fabulous" at this moderately priced wharf seafood spot; with its clean, multi-level setting, friendly service and "nice wine list", it's always "fun, especially on sunny days", and "great for weekend brunch."*

Wine Bistro at Solano Cellars* | 20 | 14 | 17 | $20 |

1580 Solano Ave. (Ordway Ave.), Albany, 525-0379

U – *Wine is the attraction at this East Bay bistro, where afficionados can sip some rare and unusual bottlings accompanied by tasty food; add moderate prices and you've got a winning combination.*

Wu Kong/SM | 22 | 18 | 18 | $25 |
1 Rincon Ctr., 101 Spear St. (Mission St.), 957-9300
M – "Superb" Shanghai cuisine served in an "elegant
ambiance" has made this Downtown Chinese a "rising
star"; "wonderful dim sum" shines at lunch, "out-of-this-
world" eggplant with mincemeat and other unusual
entrees fill out the rest of the menu; service falters if
busy, which is often.

Yamato Sukiyaki House/SM | 18 | 18 | 20 | $30 |
717 California St. (bet. Grant & Stockton Sts.), 397-3456
M – Fans say you can "always get a decent meal and
the best service" at this "old-fashioned, postwar"
Japanese, set incongruously in Chinatown; standouts
include "great sushi" and "unbelievable" chicken
teriyaki, served by kimonoed waitresses in a pleasant
and tranquil setting; critics say "ok, not memorable."

Yank Sing/S | 23 | 17 | 17 | $19 |
427 Battery St. (Clay St.), 362-1640
53 Stevenson Place (bet. 1st & 2nd Sts.), 495-4510
380 Market St. (bet. Pine & Front Sts.), 392-3888
U – Go for some of the "best dim sum in the city" at
these modern Downtown Chinese; besides a "mind-
boggling array" of dumplings, it has a "nice, clean,
contemporary" setting that's "more upscale" than at
similar establishments; all in all, "a treat for visitors"
and locals alike.

Ya Ya's | – | – | – | M |
397½ Eighth St. (Harrison St.), 255-0909
Yahya Salih, a Jeremiah Tower-Balboa Cafe alumnus,
produces Middle Eastern cuisine with a Californian
flair; though the setting is a bit too simple for a bistro
overlooking a parking lot, the very good food, including
kebabs to die for, and moderate prices keep the place
always busy.

Yet Wah/SM | 15 | 13 | 14 | $19 |
Pier 39, Embarcadero, 434-4430
2140 Clement St. (23rd Ave.), 387-8040
2019 Larkspur Landing Circle (Sir Frances Drake Blvd.),
Larkspur, 461-3631
U – Though some say this Chinese trio can be relied
upon for "good, ordinary, cheap Chinese food", most
dismiss them as a "chain on the wane", serving
"ho-hum", "Americanized" fare laced with enough
MSG to give almost anyone a headache; you can
certainly "do better", but "in a pinch", they'll suffice.

Yoshida-Ya/LSM | 22 | 21 | 18 | $24 |
2909 Webster St. (Union St.), 346-3431
U – Sit on the floor and enjoy "delicious skewers" of
hibachi-grilled goodies at San Francisco's only yakitori
bar; it also has "excellent sushi" and other Japanese
fare and "great decor to boot"; service can flounder
and "it's expensive – but Japan is, too."

Yoshi's Japanese | 18 | 16 | 17 | $22 |
Restaurant/SM
6030 Claremont Ave. (1 block west of College Ave.),
Oakland, 652-9200
M – Good sushi downstairs and even better jazz
upstairs is a winning combination at this Oakland spot;
though some liked it better before a recent remodeling
and menu change to California-Japanese, most say it's
an "unusual concept" that makes for a "great
evening"; service lapses cause one surveyor to ask if
the staff "knows what planet they're on."

Yuen Yung*/SM | 20 | 12 | 18 | $18 |
639 Santa Cruz Ave. (Doyle St.), Menlo Park, 323-7759
M – Fans of this Peninsula movie theater-turned-Chinese
restaurant praise its "excellent" clay pot chicken,
yummy pot stickers and other "terrific" food that packs
a lot of "flavor for the price"; critics say the food varies
and, at times, tastes "like it's been sitting in a warmer";
given the "abysmal" decor, you may prefer to take out.

Yuet Lee/LSMX | 22 | 4 | 12 | $19 |
1300 Stockton St. (Broadway), 982-6020
3601 26th St. (Valencia St.), 550-8998
U – Ignore the "dismal formica surroundings" and "train-
station ambiance" at this Chinatown seafood specialist
and you'll enjoy some of "the freshest", tastiest fish in
town; "clams in black bean sauce are to die for", and
the soups, squid, shrimp and other Cantonese fare are
equally "terrific" and "worth every penny"; BYO, and
"don't look in the corners or use the bathroom."

Yujean's/S | 22 | 13 | 19 | $28 |
843 San Pablo Ave. (Solano Ave.), Albany, 525-8557
U – "Great" food and wine make this modern East Bay
spot "the only Chinese worth driving 50 miles for";
fans rave about the "original" and "upscale" fare,
especially the "smoked tea duck – worthy of a national
ranking"; kudos also go to the "gracious and engaging
owners"; some complain that it's overpriced, but then,
"Shangri-la" doesn't come cheap.

Zola's/SM | 22 | 21 | 22 | $39 |

395 Hayes St. (Gough St.), 864-4824

M – Some call this romantic and elegant French (recently relocated to the Civic Center) "a find" and praise its "intense flavors", excellent wine list, "informed service" and "pretty room"; others say it "just misses": food "concepts are better than preparation" and at these prices, that's hard to swallow.

Zuni Cafe/LS | 23 | 20 | 18 | $32 |

1658 Market St. (Gough St.), 552-2522

M – "Zany" cafe is more like it; "the quintessential San Francisco restaurant", this "hip, tuned-in" Downtowner is the place "to see live hippies" and other artsy types; its "inventive" California cuisine with a Mediterranean flair sometimes misses, but often hits big, and an "excellent wine list" enhances its appeal; the funky setting is "airy and casual", the pace "fast and furious."

Zza's/LSM | 14 | 9 | 15 | $19 |

552 Grand Ave. (MacArthur St.), Oakland, 839-9124

U – "Simple but good" food, a "down-to-earth" atmosphere and "bargain" prices make this Oakland trattoria a "favorite neighborhood place" for many; it's "good for kids and loud adults", but critics note that "fun only goes so far" and sigh, "oh, it would be great if the food were better."

North of San Francisco

	F	D	S	C

AUBERGE DU SOLEIL/SM | 22 | 27 | 23 | $45 |

Auberge Du Soleil Hotel, 180 Rutherford Hill Rd.
(Silverado Trail), Rutherford, 707-963-1211
*U – "The setting and decor couldn't be more lovely"
than at this "gorgeous" wine country inn, which offers
"stupendous" vineyard views from its balcony and a
"most romantic" ambiance inside; the French food has
never been as spectacular, but word is it's "improving"
under new chef Udo Nechutneys (formerly of
Miramonte); service can falter and prices are stratospheric,
but even so, "you won't want to leave" – "stay
overnight if possible."*

Barnaby's By The Bay*/SM | 11 | 14 | 11 | $17 |

12938 Sir Francis Drake Blvd., Inverness, 669-1114
*M – Despite "quite a view", thanks to its setting on
Tomales Bay, this Marin seafood spot "never can get it
together" in the food and service departments; still,
"breakfast is excellent" and the shellfish and BBQ ribs
can be good, too, though "you can grow old waiting to
be seated."*

Brava Terrace | – | – | – | M |

3010 St. Helena Hwy. North (Lodi Lane), St. Helena,
707-963-9300
*Brand new French-American bistro in the Napa Valley
with cooking by Fred Halpert, formerly of SF Portman
Hotel; bright and airy, with friendly service and skillfully
prepared food, it's a comer that deserves watching.*

CAFE BEAUJOLAIS/SX | 25 | 20 | 22 | $27 |

961 Ukiah St. (Evergreen St.), Mendocino,
707-937-5614
*U – "Heavenly food in a homey environment without
an ounce of pretension" is the hallmark of Margaret
Fox's legendary Mendocino outpost; it specializes in
"scrumptious" breakfasts and brunches, featuring
"great breads" that are "alone worth the trip"; dinners,
though somewhat "less wonderful", are still satisfying;
it's "an oasis of good eating in a microwave desert."*

California Cafe Bar & Grill/S | 16 | 17 | 16 | $24 |

6795 Washington St. (bet. Hwy. 29 & Madison St.),
Yountville, 704-944-2330
See San Francisco Alphabetical Directory.

CHATEAU SOUVERAIN/S | 24 | 25 | 21 | $34 |

400 Souverain (Hwy. 101, Independence Lane exit),
Geyserville, 707-433-3141

*U – Dazzling Sonoma "wine country winner" featuring
the Contemporary California cooking of new chef Patricia
Windisch; her "innovative" creations make good use of
fresh, local produce; a sunny dining room with "a
fabulous view of the Alexander Valley", pleasant service
and a super wine list add to its pleasures and make it "well
worth the drive"; Sunday brunch is a special treat.*

DOMAINE CHANDON/S | 26 | 27 | 24 | $39 |

California Dr. (Hwy. 29, Veterans Home exit), Yountville,
707-944-2892

*U – One of the stars of the Napa Valley, this high-tech
winery features the "exquisite" California-French
creations of chef Philippe Jeanty, a "spectacular"
setting and "knowledgeable service – what more can
one ask?"; dishes like squab and risotto are "superb",
desserts "stupendous" and dining on the outdoor
terrace "wonderful"; prices are high, but you're getting
"the best of everything."*

Downtown Bakery and | 27 | 15 | 21 | $25 |
Creamery*/SM

308A Center St. (on the Plaza), Healdsburg, 707-431-2719
*U – Only visit this Sonoma take-out place "when you're
feeling thin" – it offers "some of the best pastry in
California", along with coffee and "terrific ice cream";
"people are known to make a meal of the sticky buns
alone" at this "French bread lovers' paradise"; you
won't mind dieting for a few days after this indulgence.*

FRENCH LAUNDRY/SX | 25 | 25 | 24 | $44 |

6640 Washington St. (Creek St.), Yountville,
707-944-2380

*U – "Rustic" Napa Valley spot that's perfect for type-B
personalities – patrons get to take leisurely strolls
through the "beautiful gardens" while waiting for the
next course to arrive; you get a "full evening and a
memorable meal", even though each night's single
menu offering may not be brilliant; some complain of
"condescending" service, but most call it a "great,
relaxed dining experience" and "very romantic."*

Grille, The/SM | – | – | – | E |

Sonoma Mission Inn, 18140 Sonoma Hwy. 12, Boyes
Hot Springs, 707-938-9000
*One of the wine country's mainstays, this tiled and
palm treed dining room at the Sonoma Mission Inn
serves up some sparkling dishes; though a bit pricey for
vineland dining, as a hotel package, it's one of the best.*

Gray Whale/SM
| – | – | – | I |

12781 Sir Francis Drake Blvd., Inverness, 669-1244
West Marin hangout that offers pizza and coffee shop food, including "good bakery items"; relaxed atmosphere and laid-back service make it pleasant for a low-key, filling meal.

JOHN ASH & CO./S
| 25 | 25 | 23 | $41 |

4330 Barnes Rd. (River Rd.), Santa Rosa, 707-527-7687
U – "One of the best in Sonoma County", this wine country spot offers "outstanding romantic dining" with fine California cuisine, "beautiful" decor and an "unsurpassed" setting; "get a table by the window so you can enjoy the scenery" or opt for "marvelous" outdoor dining; a "well-trained" staff and "great wine list" add appeal; expensive and "worth every penny."

Kenwood Restaurant/S
| 24 | 21 | 22 | $33 |

9900 Hwy. 12 (Warm Springs Rd.), Kenwood, 707-833-6326
U – "Off the beaten path but worth finding", this Sonoma spot provides outstanding California cuisine in a great Valley of the Moon setting; with "well-prepared and very satisfying" fare, "elegant" but "casual" decor and good service, it's a "best buy" and offers "quality all around"; it's especially lovely in summer when the doors are opened.

Madrona Manor/SM
| 23 | 24 | 20 | $41 |

Madrona Manor Inn, 1001 West Side Rd. (West Dry Creek Rd.), Healdsburg, 707-433-4231
M – The "imaginative" California cuisine served at this Sonoma inn is called "exquisite" by some, "pretentious" by others; likewise, the setting, in a handsome Victorian house, is either "very romantic" or "depressing", depending on whom you ask; most agree that the visiting chefs series is a "good educational experience."

MUSTARD'S GRILL/SM
| 24 | 19 | 20 | $30 |

7399 St. Helena Hwy., Yountville, 707-944-2424
U – A "great American bistro", this Napa Valley star is a "wine country must" thanks to Cindy Pawlcyn's inspired menu of fresh fish, meats and other California specialties; the "exciting" and "unique" food epitomizes "simplicity at its best" – don't miss the "heavenly baked garlic", "4-star onion rings" or spectacular creme brulee; service is "friendly and helpful" and the setting "casual", "noisy and fun"; it's no surprise that it's "always packed" – "check the obits to get a table."

PIATTI/SM | 24 | 21 | 20 | $30 |

6480 Washington St. (Oak Circle), Yountville, 707-944-2070
405 1st St. W. (Spain St.), Sonoma, 707-996-2351
*U – The "pasta, decor and service all rate A+" at this
Napa Valley country trattoria; the food is "wonderful"
and "imaginative" and the atmosphere is "very
relaxing and cheerful", with tile floors and adobe walls;
the new branch in Sonoma is said to be just as good;
very busy, so make reservations.*

Sand Dollar*/SM | 14 | 13 | 14 | $18 |

3458 Shoreline Hwy., Stinson Beach, 868-0434
*U – "Good, funky beach food" in the middle of the
Stinson Beach action in West Marin; locals like its
moderately priced seafood and beachy atmosphere, but
then "locals don't have a choice – you do"; service can
be abrupt – "do these people really want customers?"*

Starmont/SM | 23 | 26 | 21 | $36 |

Meadowood Resort, 900 Meadowood Lane (Silverado
Trail), St. Helena, 800-458-8080
*M – Though the inventive Nouvelle California cuisine
served at this "gorgeous" Napa Valley spot can be "up
and down, who cares with scenery like this?"; along
with a spectacular setting in the beautiful Meadowood
Resort, it offers "friendly" service, a "romantic"
atmosphere and "delicious" brunches; a new chef
should make this place even more of a draw.*

Station House Cafe/SM | 21 | 14 | 19 | $20 |

11285 State Hwy. 1, Point Reyes, 663-1515
*U – "The best part about going to Point Reyes is having
dinner" at this moderately priced American, which
reviewers love for its big portions of "good, plain
country food", including "chocolate devil's food cake
that's a classic"; located in an isolated seaside village,
it's worth the drive and "perfect after a hike."*

TERRA/SM | 26 | 23 | 23 | $41 |

1345 Railroad Ave. (Adams Ave.), St. Helena,
707-963-8931
*U – "A stunning surprise", this sophisticated-yet-casual
Napa Valley spot is a winner on all counts; former
Spago chef Hiroshi Sone's "refined blend of East and
West" cuisines is both "modern" and "unique", the
stone-and-wood setting epitomizes "understated
elegance", and the gracious staff charms diners with
their personal service; it's expensive, but why not – it
may be the "best in the Napa Valley."*

TRA VIGNE/S |23 | 26 | 20 |$32|
1050 Charter Oak St. (Hwy. 29), St. Helena,
707-963-4444
U – *Another winner from the Fog City-Mustard's-Bix
triumvirate, this stunning Napa Valley Northern Italian
is a "wonderful" experience, thanks to "inspired but
simple" cuisine, breezy, casual service and a lovely
setting inside and out – "sit outside on a warm night
and you'll think you're in Italy"; though some say the
food can be uneven, most dishes succeed with an
"explosion of flavors", prompting surveyors to urge
"don't miss this" – "make a trip of it."*

TRILOGY/SM |26 | 19 | 21 |$44|
1234 Main St. (Hunt St.), St. Helena, 707-963-5507
U – *"One of the majors of the valley", this tiny
(ten-table) bistro is a bit of French-California nirvana in
the Napa wine country; chef Diane Pariseau's
"beautifully prepared" dishes feature "elegant sauces
and subtle flavors" and are complemented by a
"fabulous wine list"; service and atmosphere can be
cold and somewhat pretentious, but overall, this is truly
a trilogy of good taste, looks and service.*

Vines*/SM |15 | 15 | 15 |$27|
3111 St. Helena Hwy. (Hwy. 29), St. Helena,
707-963-8991
M – *Wine country Californian that's still getting its act
together; while some say it's "getting better all the
time", others say it "used to be nicer"; pleasant for
lunch, but "don't sit out on the balcony – noisy."*

South of San Francisco

F	D	S	C

Abalonetti/SM | 12 | 7 | 13 | $15 |

57 Old Fisherman's Wharf, Monterey, 408-373-1851
*M – Some say this "down-home" Monterey Italian
provides "good, inexpensive seafood"; others say it
serves "beaucoup de grease" and call it "a variation on
'cheezburga', with squid instead"; either way, its
"easy" atmosphere, low prices and friendly service
make it "good for kids", and nice bay views distract
from the "grim surroundings."*

Adriatic Restaurant*/S | 19 | 16 | 22 | $37 |

14583 Big Basin Way (5th St.), Saratoga, 408-867-3110
*M – Some say this "intimate" and romantic South Bay
Continental exudes "class" with its "very well-prepared
food" and "attentive, unobtrusive" service; others call
it a "letdown" that's "too expensive"; all agree on its
appeal for "warm lingering."*

Alexander's/SM | - | - | - | E |

Marriott Hotel, Mission College Blvd. (Great American
Pkwy.), Santa Clara, 408-988-4300
*Though "nothing spectacular", this attractive South Bay
Continental offers an elegant, dark-paneled setting and
"good", if somewhat predictable, food; service is
professional and friendly.*

Australian Restaurant/SMX | - | - | - | M |

898 Lincoln Ave. (Paula Ave.), San Jose, 408-293-1112
*Lively San Jose spot that offers Eclectic food from
Down Under; although not brilliant, the food is decent
and inexpensive, and the atmosphere is casual and
lighthearted enough for Crocodile Dundee to enjoy;
service, on the other hand, is described as "standoffish."*

Baccarat Room*/M | 17 | 21 | 14 | $39 |

Hotel Sofitel, 223 Twin Dolphin Dr. (Shoreline Dr.),
Redwood City, 598-9000
*U – "Pretentious" and "disappointing" sum up the
reactions to this fancy hotel dining room – both food
and ambiance are "stiffly French" and the bill is very
high; "I don't like having my French pronunciation
corrected by the staff."*

South of San Francisco | F | D | S | C |

Barbarossa/SM | 20 | 18 | 22 | $36 |
3003 El Camino Real (East Selby Lane), Redwood City, 369-2626
U – Fans say this "romantic" chef-owned Peninsula Continental is an example of "European style at its near best" with "solid" cuisine, smooth service and a "warm, friendly" atmosphere that always "hits a homer"; the "excellent prix fixe menus" are a good deal.

Beau Sejour/SM | 21 | 19 | 16 | $31 |
170 State St. (3rd St.), Los Altos, 948-1388
Le Parisien
327 Lorton Ave., Burlingame, 343-9433
U – Peninsula siblings offering Nouvelle cuisine with an interesting Vietnamese twist; the food is "imaginative" and "can be great", especially when the chef is in the kitchen – don't miss the duck with raspberry sauce; Los Altos "is prettier", but both have a "lovely atmosphere."

California Cafe Bar & Grill/S | 16 | 17 | 16 | $24 |
Stanford Barn, 700 Welch Rd. (Quarry St.), Palo Alto, 325-2233
Valley Fair Shopping Ctr., 2855 Stevens Creek Blvd., Santa Clara, 408-296-2233
5925 Almaden Expwy., San Jose, 408-268-2233
855 E. Homestead Rd. (Wolfe St.), Sunnyvale, 408-739-7670
See San Francisco Alphabetical Directory.

Casanova* | 23 | 24 | 20 | $29 |
Fifth St. (bet. San Carlos & Misson Sts.), Carmel, 408-625-0501
U – "Quaint" Monterey area Northern Italian that gets high marks for "comfortable surroundings", a "very European" atmosphere, consistent food and smooth service; one surveyor calls it "Carmel's most romantic restaurant."

Central 159/SM | - | - | - | E |
159 Central Ave., Pacific Grove, 408-372-2235
Superb California cuisine created by chef David Beckwith who used to work his magic at Rio Grill; bright, attractive and low-key, don't miss the roasted garlic, lobster quesadilla, fettuna (a baby pizza) and grilled rabbit; the food and charming service make it worth the trip.

South of San Francisco | F | D | S | C |

Chaminade*/S | 19 | 21 | 17 | $30 |

1 Chaminade Lane (Paul Sweet Rd.), Santa Cruz,
408-475-5600
*U – "Elegant" Santa Cruz oceanside spot that offers
Continental food in a sedate library setting; the Sunday
brunch and Friday night seafood buffet get the highest
marks, but food is generally called "very good"; the
"view is great" but prices can be steep.*

Chantilly Francais/S | – | – | – | E |

530 Ramona St. (bet. University & Hamilton Aves.),
Palo Alto, 321-4080
*Peninsula haute French that earns high marks for
"excellent, if not innovative, food"; the surroundings
are attractive but service can be "officious"; bring
plenty of money.*

Chef Chu's | 20 | 12 | 14 | $19 |

1067 N. San Antonio Rd. (El Camino St.), Los Altos,
948-2696
*M – Popular Peninsula Chinese that's "still very good,
but less so than before – is this the price of fame?"; still,
most reviewers call it "one of the better Chinese in the
Bay Area" with "creative and different" food and "an
almost-French touch" to its sauces; a recent face-lift has
improved the ambiance, but service is utilitarian and
somewhat "impersonal."*

Chez T. J. | 25 | 21 | 20 | $45 |

938 Villa St. (bet. Baily & Castro Sts.), Mountain View,
964-7466
*M – "Innovative", ofttimes "amazing", California-French
cuisine served in a "very quaint" Victorian setting;
though some are put off by the "stuffy, humorless"
service and "pretentious" attitude, most call it one of
the "best of the Peninsula" with a good wine list and
nice "European style."*

Clark's by the Bay | 12 | 17 | 14 | $24 |

487 Seaport Court (Seaport Blvd.), Redwood City,
367-9222
*U – "Football groupies" hardly notice the "mediocre"
American food served at this popular Peninsula
bar/restaurant – they're too busy trying to catch a
glimpse of owner Dwight Clark, ex-49er wide receiver,
and his jock buddies; with a "lovely view" and "great
bar", it's a good place to drink or catch a game, not dine.*

South of San Francisco | F | D | S | C |

COVEY RESTAURANT, THE*/S | 24 | 24 | 22 | $42 |
Quail Lodge, 8205 Valley Green Dr. (Carmel Valley Rd.),
Carmel, 408-624-1581
U – Attractive Monterey area restaurant in the beautiful
Carmel Valley; the decor is "lovely" and the Continental
food is nicely prepared; big with the golfing set, it's
pricey but offers very good quality.

Crow's Nest/SM | 13 | 19 | 14 | $20 |
2218 E. Cliff Dr. (Lake St.), Santa Cruz, 408-476-4560
U – Undistinguished family fish house with distinguished
views of the Santa Cruz waterfront; it's best simply "to
sit on the balcony, have a drink and watch the sailboats
come in."

El Maghreb/S | – | – | – | M |
145 W. Santa Clara St. (San Pedro St.), San Jose,
408-294-2243
South Bay Moroccan that blends exotic North
African food with sinewy belly dancers; the tented
dining room offers a seven-course feast that's
delicious as well as a "fun dining experience";
service is attentive and prices moderate.

EMILE'S | 26 | 22 | 25 | $40 |
545 S. 2nd St. (Williams St.), San Jose, 408-289-1960
U – South Bay institution featuring the cooking of
chef-owner Emile Mooser, a Swiss with classical French
training; "San Jose's best restaurant" turns out
"top-notch", "classic" Continental cuisine which, a few
feel, "needs updating"; though "a little cramped", the
setting is attractive and service professional, adding to
an overall "outstanding" experience.

Enoteca Mastro | 22 | 14 | 21 | $29 |
933 San Pablo Ave. (bet. Marin & Solano Aves.),
Albany, 524-4822
U – "Refreshing, new" East Bay Northern Italian that
offers "really authentic" food that is "scholarly and
brave"; pick your wine from the next door enoteca,
then settle into a "very interesting" meal that might
include "lovely Tuscan pastas" and "great antipasti";
"crowded, upbeat" and "very friendly."

110

Eulipia | 22 | 20 | 19 | $30 |

374 S. 1st St. (bet. San Carlos & San Salvador Sts.),
San Jose, 408-280-6161
U – "Casual, chic and friendly" South Bay bistro/trattoria
featuring "definitive California cuisine" that's "creative"
and "fresh" – try the Chinese chicken salad and
desserts; "service could be faster", especially at busy
lunchtime, but you can while away the time looking at
some interesting art on display.

FRESH CREAM/S | 27 | 23 | 25 | $39 |

99 Pacific St., Ste. 100F (Heritage Harbor), Monterey,
408-375-9798
U – Fancy Monterey French that gets fabulous ratings in
every category; fans call it "one of the best in Northern
California" with rich food that's "an orgasm for the
tongue"; "it's hard to watch your cholesterol here",
given such dishes as "fabulous duck in black sauce"
and trout in browned butter; "lovely" service and a
"very relaxing" atmosphere add to what, by all reports,
is a "wonderful" experience.

Fung Lum | 18 | 22 | 16 | $21 |

1815 S. Bascom Ave. (bet. Hamilton & Campbell Aves.),
Campbell, 408-377-6955
U – "Outstanding decor" is the main asset of this South
Bay Chinese; its Hong Kong-style food is "good but
overpriced for what you get", though the "minced
squab is a real treat"; "beware of wedding receptions"
and "waiters rude enough to work at the Wharf."

Gervais/M | 24 | 18 | 25 | $32 |

1798 Park Ave. (Neglee St.), San Jose, 408-275-8631
U – Fancy South Bay French that offers extremely
well-crafted, but somehow undramatic, food; the
presentations are eye-catching and the service is
pleasant, but as for the decor, "its tackiness makes the
place adorable."

Giuliano's*/S | 26 | 23 | 21 | $39 |

Mission Ave. (5th St.), Carmel, 408-625-5231
U – The ratings keep soaring for this intimate and
romantic Monterey area Italian; some say it offers "the
best Italian food in Carmel", along with a charming
ambiance and attentive, but unobtrusive, service; "a
great little find."

Il Fornaio/LSM | 21 | 23 | 18 | $27 |

223 Corte Madera Town Ctr., Corte Madera, 927-4400
Garden Court Hotel, 520 Cowper St., Palo Alto,
408-332-9000

M – "Very Italiana", this trio of instant "in" spots earns
raves for stylish looks and "chic", "sophisticated"
ambiance, and mostly plaudits for the Northern Italian
fare, especially the "fabulous" pastas and breads; even
detractors are impressed by the "designer decor" ("is
there any marble left in Italy?"); sore points accompany
popularity – sometimes "inept" service, crowds and
noise; P.S. "excellent for breakfast", too.

J.R. Chops*/M | 16 | 17 | 18 | $28 |

2106 El Camino Real (Scott Blvd.), Santa Clara,
408-244-3700

U – South Bay steakhouse that's a "good place for a
red-meat fix at reasonable prices"; while some say it's
one of "the best in that part of town", critics say it's
"already seen its heyday and is on the decline."

La Foret*/S | 21 | 22 | 22 | $36 |

21747 Bertram Rd. (S. Almaden Expwy.), San Jose,
408-997-3458

M – Some say this pricey San Jose Continental is
"nothing special" and "needs some imagination";
others say it's got "class written all over it" and is
"worth the expedition to get there" for good food and
service ("just don't let them stick you in the dining
room upstairs"); it's a nice outing for Sunday brunch.

La Mere Michelle*/SM | 21 | 20 | 22 | $42 |

14467 Big Basin Way (3rd St.), Saratoga, 408-867-5272

M – Pricey South Bay French that's one of the better
Peninsula stops, thanks to good, if "heavy", haute
cuisine and "impeccable" service; "incredible" desserts
get special praise, as does the "lovely, quiet" ambiance;
critics say it's "riding on its reputation."

LE MOUTON NOIR/SM | 25 | 23 | 24 | $42 |

14560 Big Basin Way (bet. 4th & 5th Sts.), Saratoga,
408-867-7017

U – With few exceptions, this pricey South Bay French is
praised as a star of the region – "the best French
restaurant in Santa Clara County"; try the pancakes and
caviar appetizer, the souffles, seafood and duck; a "quaint
romantic setting" in a lovely Victorian house and caring
service help make it "perfect for every occasion."

South of San Francisco | F | D | S | C |

Le Papillon/SM | 24 | 20 | 22 | $34 |
410 Saratoga Ave. (Keily Blvd.), San Jose, 408-296-3730
M – Expensive, San Jose haute French power lunch spot (and sister of La Foret) that fans call "one of the best" – "can't think of a thing I'd change"; critics knock the "stuffy" atmosphere and say "food is good but not commensurate with price."

L'Escale*/SM | 18 | 19 | 20 | $23 |
5 Stanford Shopping Ctr. (El Camino Real), Palo Alto, 326-9857
U – "Good French food", a "small, cozy" setting and pleasant service make this South Bay bistro in the Stanford Shopping Center a good choice for lunch or dinner; it may not be very exciting, but it is "very enjoyable."

Les Saisons* | 25 | 27 | 26 | $45 |
Fairmont Hotel, 170 S. Market St. (1st St.), San Jose, 408-998-3950
U – "Wonderful" Contemporary American food and an "elegant", "beautiful" setting make this pricey hotel dining room "a treat for all seasons"; it's a good special-occasion spot, though some find it "too formal and posh" and say that service can be "intrusive."

L'Horizon Restaurant/M | – | – | – | E |
1250 Aviation Ave. (Coleman Ave.), San Jose, 408-295-1771
South Bay French in an obscure location that seems to be slipping; the food is unmemorable, decor simple and service erratic.

Library, The | – | – | – | E |
1 Chaminade Lane (Hwy. 1), Santa Cruz, 408-475-2509
The food gets high marks at this romantic Santa Cruz spot, though some say it's too self-conscious and, like most ambitious places outside the city, "needs to relax"; prix fixe menu is a good deal in an otherwise expensive place.

Lion and Compass/M | 18 | 19 | 18 | $33 |
1023 N. Fair Oaks Ave. (Hwy. 101), Sunnyvale, 408-745-1260
M – "Still the place to be seen in Silicon Valley", but this pricey South Bay American would probably qualify as "ordinary in the city"; the food is "fairly reliable if unexciting", though to critics it "tastes like silicon" and is overpriced to boot; a popular power lunch spot, it's "uncrowded at dinner."

Osteria/M | 22 | 17 | 19 | $26 |
247 Hamilton Ave. (Ramona Ave.), Palo Alto, 328-5700
M – No fireworks here, but these casual, moderately priced trattorias provide "good Italian food in an authentic ambiance"; favorite dishes include spaghetti carbonara and calamari mugnaia; some complain that the San Francisco restaurant is too small and tables too close together, but they're both "bustling and fun" with friendly service.

Pacific Fresh/S | 16 | 15 | 14 | $24 |
1130 N. Mathilda Ave. (Lockheed Way), Sunnyvale,
408-745-1710
550 Ellenwood Way (Ellenwood Dr.), Pleasanthill,
827-3474
21255 Stevens Creek Hwy. (Bubb Rd.), Cupertino,
408-252-5311
M – Peninsula seafood places that have split surveyors between those who praise the "good, basic seafood" at "decent prices" and those who call the food "disappointing and ill-prepared"; they must be doing something right since "they're loud and a wait is usually in store."

Palermo*/SM | 22 | 10 | 18 | $28 |
380 S. 2nd St. (San Carlos Ave.), San Jose,
408-297-0607
M – If you can't make it to Gilroy, try this moderately priced, no-decor San Jose Sicilian for "good, garlicky food": "awesome caprese" and "fresh and incredibly delicious" pastas; it's a "warm, hospitable place", though the staff "has trouble handling crowds."

Paolo's*/M | 23 | 16 | 20 | $33 |
520 E. Santa Clara St. (bet. 11th & 12th Sts.), San
Jose, 408-294-2558
U – South Bay Continental that gets high marks for food and, in the past, was panned for its seedy location, in the process of moving as we go to press; if the food stays the same and the ambiance improves, this could be a real find.

Plumed Horse, The/LM | 22 | 22 | 23 | $38 |
14555 Big Basin Way (4th St.), Saratoga, 408-867-4711
M – Some praise this pricey Peninsula French-Continental for its "excellent Country French food", "lovely" decor and outstanding wine list; others call it "steady but unspectacular" and say, "too fancy – fake red velvet isn't our style"; it "never changes", which pleases its fans and dismays its critics.

RIO GRILL/SM | 22 | 20 | 20 | $29 |

Crossroads Shopping Ctr., 101 Crossroads Blvd. (Rio Rd.),
Carmel Valley, 408-625-5436

*M – Though some say food quality has dipped since
the departure of chef Cindy Pawlcyn, most still consider
this the definitive Monterey-area California cuisine
mecca; its clever regional and Southwest-accented menu
offers some of the "best food in Carmel", and the good
wine list and crisp, modern decor draw praise as well;
given its popularity, service can be "as slow as fog."*

San Benito House/S | 19 | 21 | 19 | $28 |

356 Main St. (Mill St.), Half Moon Bay, 726-3425

*M – You can count on the beautiful garden setting and
cozy, romantic atmosphere at this moderately priced
Peninsula Mediterranean, but not on the "inconsistent"
food; it succeeds often enough, though, for some to
dub it "a sparkling blue jewel on Highway One" that's
"worth the drive"; go early, since they may run out of
the more popular entrees.*

Sardine Factory/LSM | 20 | 21 | 20 | $37 |

701 Wave St. (Prescott St.), Monterey, 408-373-3775

*M – Surveyors either love (the majority) or hate (the
minority) this expensive, overwrought Italian restaurant
in Monterey; "you can have a wonderful meal here" say
its many fans, who find the "Disneyland" decor amusing;
others see it as a "pretentious, overrated tourist trap"
with "garish bordello decor"; the wine list is excellent
and, as ratings show, this is a well-oiled operation.*

Scott's Seafood Grill | 18 | 17 | 17 | $26 |
and Bar/SM

2300 E. Bayshore Rd. (bet. East & Embarcadero Sts.),
Palo Alto, 856-1046

See San Francisco Alphabetical Directory.

Sinaloa/SX | – | – | – | M |

19210 Monterey Hwy. (Peebles Ave.), Morgan Hill,
408-779-9740

*Great margaritas and authentic Mexican food explain
the appeal of this inexpensive South Bay joint; chili
Colorado and chili verde are among the favorites,
served with a steaming stack of flour or corn tortillas;
come early and be prepared to wait on weekends; there's
no atmosphere, but with enough tequila, who cares?*

South of San Francisco

Sue's Kitchen*/SM

| 22 | 8 | 18 | $16 |

1061 E. El Camino Rd. (Henderson St.), Sunnyvale,
408-296-6522
U – Reviewers love the authentic Indian home cooking
at this inexpensive South Bay spot; it's an "incredible
value" and, some say, "as good as upscale places
costing much more"; don't expect much in the way of
decor, but service is friendly.

Swedish Place/SM

| 19 | 16 | 16 | $27 |

2320 S. Cabrillo Hwy., Half Moon Bay, 726-7322
M – "Homey" oceanside Peninsula "gem" that
specializes in cream-sauced fish dishes and other
moderately priced Scandinavian fare; "charming but
heavy", it's nicest for Sunday brunch and Thursday
night buffet; "be prepared for the co-ed bathroom."

Taco Al Pastor/SX

| – | – | – | I |

400 S. Bascone Ave. (bet. San Carlos & Moore Park),
San Jose, 408-275-1619
Bare-bones South Bay Mexican that offers "good,
greasy Tex-Mex" fare in a spartan environment; it's not
much on service or decor, but what do you expect from
what may be the cheapest place in the Survey.

Teske's Germania*

| 17 | 18 | 19 | $22 |

255 N. 1st St. (bet. St. James & Julian Aves.), San Jose,
408-292-0291
M – Large portions and moderate prices are the main
attributes of this South Bay German spot; though
authentic, the food doesn't inspire much enthusiasm
among reviewers ("did not remind me much of
Munich"); still, a good plate of saurbraten and
gemutlich service keep 'em coming back.

Victorian Garden Restaurant

| – | – | – | M |

476 S. 1st St. (Williams St.), San Jose, 408-286-1770
Charming, kitschy South Bay Continental with Italian
influences; "great" is the favorite adjective, repeatedly
applied as a prefix to "atmosphere" and "garden", but
not to the service.

INDEXES TO
RESTAURANTS

SPECIAL FEATURES
AND APPEALS

TYPES OF CUISINE*

Afghan

Helmand

American

American Chow
Avenue Grill
Barnaby's By The Bay/N
Betty's Ocean Diner
Big Four
Bill's Place
Blue Light Cafe
Brazen Head
Butler's
Cafe Beaujolais/N
Cafe 222
California Cafe Bar & Grill
Caprice, The
Carnelian Room
Clement St. Bar/Grill
Crow's Nest/S
Dipsea Cafe
Doidge's Kitchen
Eddie Rickenbacher's
Embarko
Fat Apple's
Hamburger Mary's
Hard Rock Cafe
Harpoon Louie's
Harris' Restaurant
House of Prime Rib
Ironwood Cafe
Ivy's
Izzy's Steak/Chop Hse.
Lion and Compass/S
Lori's Diner
Mama's
Mama's Royal Cafe
Max's Diner
Max's Opera Cafe
Mel's Diner
Mo's
Palm, The
Paloma
Perry's
Sally's
Sam's Grill
Sears Fine Foods
Stanford Park

Station House Cafe/N
Tommy's Joynt
Triple Rock Brewery

American New

Asta
Bix
Brava Terrace/N
Cafe For All Seasons
Campton Place
Casa Madrona
Clark's by the Bay/S
Courtyard, The
El Drisco Hotel
Faz Restaurant/Bar
John Ash & Co./N
Kenwood Restaurant/N
Lark Creek Inn, The
Pier 23 Cafe
Plumed Horse, The/S

Australian

Australian Restaurant/S

Austrian

Hyde St. Bistro

Bar-B-Q

Barnaby's By The Bay/N
Doug's BBQ
Faz Rest. Bar & Grill
Hahn's Hibachi
King Charcoal BBQ Hse.
MacArthur Park
San Francisco BBQ

Brazilian

Bahia
DePaula's Restaurant

Burmese

Mandalay
Nan Yang

---

*All restaurants are in the San Francisco metropolitan area
unless otherwise noted. "S" indicates South of San Francisco
and "N" indicates North of San Francisco.

Cajun/Creole

Elite Cafe, The
Gulf Coast Oyster Bar
Regina's

Californian

Ace Cafe
A la Carte
Auberge du Soleil/N
Augusta's
Balboa Cafe
Bay Wolf
Butler's
Cafe at Chez Panisse
Cafe Beaujolais/N
Cafe Fanny
California Cafe Bar & Grill
Campbell House
Central/S
Chateau Souverain/N
Chez Panisse
Christopher's
City Block
Cliff House
Courtyard, The
Curbside Cafe
Domaine Chandon/N
Eddie Jacks
Eulipia/S
565 Clay
Flea Street Cafe
Flying Saucer
Fog City Diner
Fourth Street Grill
French Laundry/N
Grille, The/N
Hayes Street Grill
Horizons
Island Cafe
Ivy's
John Ash & Co./N
Julie's Supper Club
Lafayette on Pacific
Lalime's
L'Avenue
Lehr's Greenhouse
Library, The/S
London Wine Bar, The
Madrona Manor/N
Miss Pearl's Jam House
Mustard's Grill/N
Narsai's Cafe
Norman's Restaurant
Omnivore
Pacific Grill
Panama Hotel
Park Grill

Pixley Cafe
Postrio
Rio Grill/S
Rotunda, The
Santa Fe Bar/Grill
Savannah Grill
Silks
690
South Park Cafe
Splendido's
Stanford Park
Starmont/N
Stars
Terra/N
Thornhill Cafe
Trilogy/N
Victor's
Vines/N
Washington Sq. Bar/Grill
Ya Ya's
Zuni Cafe

Cambodian

Angkor Palace
Angkor Wat
Bayon, The
Cambodia House
Phnom Penh

Caribbean

Caribbean Zone
Geva's
Miss Pearl's Jam House
690

Chinese

Brandy Ho's
Celadon
Chef Chu's/S
China Moon Cafe
China Pavilion
China Station
Chu Lin
Empress of China
Feng Nian
Flower Lounge
Fook, The
Fountain Court
Fung Lum/S
Golden Phoenix
Harbor Village
Hong Kong Tea House
House of Nanking
Hunan Restaurant
Imperial Palace
Jade Villa

Jin Jiang Kee Joon
Kan's
King of China
Kirin
Lychee Garden
Mandarin, The
Mandarin House
Mike's Chinese Cuisine
Monsoon
Narai
North Sea Village
Ocean City
Ocean Restaurant
Ping Yuen
South China Cafe
Straits Cafe
Taiwan Restaurant
Tien Fu
Tommy Toy's Chinoise
Ton Kiang
Tung Fong
Uncle Yu's
Vegi Food
Wu Kong
Yank Sing
Yet Wah
Yuen Yung
Yuet Lee
Yujean's

Coffee Houses

Bohemian Cigar Store
Cafe Greco
Caffe Roma
Cheer's Cafe
Curbside Cafe
Downtown Bakery/N
Gray Whale/N
Mama's
Mama's Royal Cafe
Miz Brown's Feed Bag
Trio Cafe

Continental

Act IV
Adriatic
Adriatic Restaurant
Alexander's/S
Alta Mira Restaurant
Barbarossa/S
Beethoven
Bella Vista
Big Four
Cafe De Bordeaux
Cafe Majestic
Cafe Mozart
Caprice, The
Castagnola's

Chambord
Chaminade/S
Covey Restaurant/S
Dal Baffo
El Paseo
Fly Trap Restaurant
Fournou's Oven
French Room, The
Iron Horse, The
Jack's
J.R. Chops/S
Julius' Castle
La Foret/S
La Petite Auberge
Lascaux
Les Saisons/S
Mirabelle
Nadine's
1001 Nob Hill Rest.
Sardine Factory/S
Schroeder's
Squid's Cafe
Squire Restaurant
Tourelle
Trader Vic's
Vanessi's
Victorian Garden Rest./S
Vlasta's European

Cuban

Cha Cha Cha's
Cuba

Czechoslovakian

Vlasta's European

Delis

Acropolis Deli
Brother's Delicatessen
Max's Opera Cafe
Moishe's Pipick
Saul's Delicatessen
Vivande Porta Via

Dim Sum

Celadon
China Moon Cafe
Flower Lounge
Fook, The
Harbor Village
Hong Kong Tea House
Jade Villa
King of China
Ocean City
Tung Fong
Wu Kong
Yank Sing

Diners

American Chow
Betty's Ocean Diner
Bricks
Carrera's
Fog City Diner
Lori's Diner
Mama's
Mama's Royal Cafe
Max's Diner
Mel's Diner
Miz Brown's Feed Bag
Sears Fine Foods

Eclectic

Asta
Barnaby's By The Bay/N
Caprice, The
Chez Panisse
Diamond St. Rest.
French Laundry/N
Guernica
L'Avenue
Little City Antipasti Bar
Madrona Manor/N
Oritalia
Panama Hotel
San Benito House/S
Square One
Thornhill Cafe
Trader Vic's

French Bistro

A la Carte
Brasserie Tomo
Calif. Culinary Academy
Chambord
Christophe
Guernica
Kenwood Restaurant/N
Lalime's
Lascaux
Le Central
Le Cyrano
Le Metropole
L'Entrecote de Paris
Le Piano Zinc
L'Escale/S
Le St. Tropez
Le Trou Restaurant
Old Swiss House
South Park Cafe
Zola's

French Classic

Act IV
Auberge du Soleil/N

Baccarat Room/S
Barbarossa/S
Cafe Mozart
Calif. Culinary Academy
Chez T.J./S
Emile's/S
Ernie's
Fleur de Lys
Gervais/S
Jack's
La Folie
La Foret/S
La Mere Duquesne
La Mere Michelle/S
La Petite Auberge
Le Castel
Le Club
Le Marquis
Le Papillon/S
L'Escargot
Masa's
Monroe's
Nob Hill Restaurant
Pierre at Meridien
Rue de Main
Tourelle
231 Ellsworth

French Nouvelle

Amelio's
Beau Sejour/S
Brava Terrace/N
Campbell House
Domaine Chandon/N
Fleur de Lys
Janot's
Le Castel
Le Domino
Le Marquis
Le Mouton Noir/S
L'Horizon Restaurant/S
Masa's
Nob Hill Restaurant
Pierre at Meridien
Regina's
Rodin
Shadows, The
Silks
Starmont/N
Tourelle
Trilogy/N

German

Beethoven
Cafe Mozart
Schroeder's
Teske's Germania/S

Greek

S. Asimakopoulous

Grills

Avenue Grill
Clement St. Bar/Grill
Corona Bar/Grill
Grille, The
Hayes Street Grill
MacArthur Park
Maltese Grill
Mustard's Grill/N
Pacific Grill
Pacific Hts. Bar/Grill
Sam's Grill
Santa Fe Bar/Grill
Savannah Grill
Scott's Seafood Grill/S
Sedona Grill/Bar
Spiedini
Stars
Tadich Grill
Washington Sq. Bar/Grill
Yoshida-Ya

Hamburgers

Balboa Cafe
Bill's Place
Bricks
Cheer's Cafe
Clement St. Bar/Grill
Fat Apple's
Fog City Diner
Hamburger Mary's
Hard Rock Cafe
Lori's Diner
Mel's Diner
Original Joe's
Perry's

Hungarian

Paprika's Fono

Indian

Gaylord Restaurant
Himalaya Restaurant
India House
Indian Oven
Mela
North India Rest.
Sue's Kitchen/S

Indonesian

Java Restaurant
Straits Cafe

Italian

Abalonetti/S
A. Sabella's
Bella Voce
Bohemian Cigar Store
Bonta
Bruno's
Buca Giovani
Bucci's
Caffe Roma
Caffe Venezia
Capp's Corner
Carrera's
Franco's
Giramonti
Il Pirata
Iron Horse, The
Lanzone Alexander
La Traviata
La Fiammetta Ristorante
Little City Antipasti Bar
Little Henry's
Little Italy
Lucca Ristorante
Marin Joe's
Original Joe's
Paolo's/S
Pasta Moon
Piatti/N
Pietro's
Riera's
Ristorante Grifone
Ruby's
Sardine Factory/S
Spuntino
Tarantino's
Ti Bacio
Tommaso's
Trattoria Contadina
Undici
U.S. Restaurant
Vanessi's
Viareggio
Victorian Garden Rest./S
Vivande Porta Via
Zza's

Italian (Northern)

Adriana's
Alessia
Baci
Bardelli's
Basta Pasta
Blue Fox, The
Cafe Riggio
Carlo's Restaurant
Casanova/S
Chez Panisse

Donatello
Enoteca Lanzone
Enoteca Mastro/S
Etrusca
Fior d'Italia
Giuliano's/S
Hyde St. Bistro
I Fratelli
Il Fornaio
Kuleto's
Laghi
La Pergola
Little Joe's
Mescolanza
Milano Joe's
Milano Pizzeria
New Joe's
New San Remo
North Beach Restaurant
Olivetto
Osteria
Parma
Prego Ristorante
Ristorante Fabrizio
Ristorante Milano
Spiedini
Terra/N
Tra Vigne/N
Umberto's

Italian (Southern)

Cafe Riggio
Caffe Sport
Circolo
Ernesto's
Jackson Fillmore
La Ginestra
Little Italy
Palermo/S
Via Veneto

Italian (Nuova Cucina)

Acqurello
Alessia
Blue Fox, The
Kuleto's
Mescolanza
Ristorante Milano
Tutto Bene

Japanese

Benihana
Ebisu
Edokko
Goro's Robato
Isobune Sushi
Kabuto Sushi

Kansai
Kirala
Mifune
Mikado
Mitoya
Osome
Samurai
Sanppo
Tanuki
Yamato Sukiyaki Hse.
Yoshida-Ya
Yoshi's Rest.

Jewish

Moishe's Pipick†
Saul's Delicatessen†
Shenson's*†
(*Not in *Survey*)
(† Serves Kosher food)

Korean

Hahn's Hibachi
King Charcoal BBQ Hse.
Kirin
Korea House
Seoul Garden

Mexican

Alejandro's Sociedad
Cactus Cafe
Cadillac Bar & Rest.
Cantina, The
Casa Aguila
Chevys
Corona Bar/Grill
Don Ramon's
El Sombrero
El Tapatio
El Tazumal
Guaymas
Juan's Place
La Mexicana
La Rondalla
La Taqueria
Leticia's
Los Chiles
Mom is Cooking
Roosevelt Tamale
Sinaloa/S
Taco Al Pastor/S
Taqueria Mission
Tortola Restaurant

Mediterranean

Maltese Grill
San Benito House/S
Splendido's

123

Square One
Wine Bistro/Solano
Zola's
Zuni Cafe

Middle Eastern

Cairo Cafe
La Mediterranee
Middle East Restaurant
Ya Ya's

Moroccan

Citrus Grill
El Maghreb/S
Mamounia
Marrakech Moroccan
Pasha

Nicaraguan

Nicaragua Restaurant

Oyster Bars

Bentley's
Gulf Coast Oyster Bar
La Rocca's Oyster Bar
Maye's Oyster House
Pacific Hts. Bar/Grill
Swan Oyster Depot

Persian

Casablanca

Philippine

Barrio Fiesta

Pizza

Bucci's
Cafe at Chez Panisse
Caffe Sport
Cheer's Cafe
Circolo
DePaula's Restaurant
Ernesto's
Gray Whale/N
Il Fornaio
Little Henry's
Milano Pizzeria
Olivetto
Postrio
Prego Ristorante
Ruby's
Spuntino
Tommaso's
Vicolo Pizzeria
Zza's

Polynesian

Trader Vic's

Russian

Acropolis Deli

Salvadorean

El Tazumal
La Roca Restaurant

Seafood

Abalonetti/S
Adriatic
Alioto's Restaurant
A. Sabella's
Augusta's
Bentley's
Castagnola's
Cliff House
Crow's Nest/S
Ebisu
Flower Lounge
Flynn's Landing
Gertie's Chesapeake Bay
Gulf Coast Oyster Bar
Hayes Street Grill
Horizons
La Roca Restaurant
La Rocca's Oyster Bar
Long Life Vegi House
Maye's Oyster House
Ocean Restaurant
Omnivore
Original Old Clam Hse.
Osome
Pacific Cafe
Pacific Fresh
Pacific Hts. Bar/Grill
Ronayne's
Sam's Anchor Cafe
Sam's Grill
Sand Dollar/N
Savoy Brasserie
Scoma's
Scott's Seafood Grill/S
Spenger's Fish Grotto
Squid's Cafe
Swan Oyster Depot
Tadich Grill
Trader Vic's
Viareggio
Waterfront Restaurant

Southwestern

Cactus Cafe
Fourth Street Grill

Sedona Grill/Bar
Tortola Restaurant

Spanish

Alejandro's Sociedad
Los Chiles
Maltese Grill

Steakhouses

Alfred's
Crow's Nest/S
Eulipia/S
Harris' Restaurant
House of Prime Rib
Izzy's Steak/Chop Hse.
Original Joe's

Swedish

Swedish Place/S

Swiss

Ernie's
Old Swiss House

Thai

Dusit Thai
Khan Toke Thai House

Manora's Thai Cuisine
Narai
Ploy Thai
Plearn Thai Cuisine
Ploy Thai
Royal Thai
Samui
San Francisco BBQ
Siam Cuisine
Thep Phanom

Vegetarian

Diamond St. Rest.
565 Clay
Green's
Long Life Vegi House
Milly's
Vegi Food

Vietnamese

Aux Delices
Beau Sejour/S
Cordon Bleu Vietnamese
Emerald Garden
Golden Turtle
Kim's
Mai's
Mekong
Tu Lan

NEIGHBORHOOD LOCATIONS

Castro/Noe

Diamond St. Rest.
La Roca Restaurant
Le Piano Zinc
Leticia's
Little Italy
South China Cafe

Chinatown

Celadon
Empress of China
Golden Phoenix
Helmand
Hong Kong Tea House
House of Nanking
Hunan Restaurant
Imperial Palace
Kan's
Lychee Garden
Ocean City
Ping Yuen
Tung Fong
Yamato Sukiyaki Hse.
Yuet Lee

Civic Center

Act IV
Calif. Culinary Academy
Enoteca Lanzone
Hayes Street Grill
Ivy's
Max's Opera Cafe
Moishe's Pipick
690
Spuntino
Stars
Stars Cafe
Vicolo Pizzeria
Zuni Cafe

Downtown

Bardelli's
Bentley's
Big Four
Bix
Blue Fox, The
Cafe Claude
Cafe Mozart
Cafe 222
Campton Place
Carnelian Room
Chambord
China Moon Cafe
Circolo
Corona Bar/Grill
Donatello
Ernie's
Faz Restaurant/Bar
565 Clay
Fleur de Lys
Fog City Diner
Geva's
Harbor Village
India House
Iron Horse, The
Isobune Sushi
Jack's
Janot's
Julius' Castle
Kansai
Kuleto's
Lafayette on Pacific
La Mere Duquesne
Lascaux
Le Central
L'Olivier
London Wine Bar, The
Lori's Diner
Los Chiles
MacArthur Park
Maltese Grill
Mama's
Marrakech Moroccan
Masa's
Mela
Mo's
Narsai's Cafe
New Joe's
Original Joe's
Pacific Grill
Park Grill
Pierre at Meridien
Pier 23 Cafe
Regina's
Ristorante Milano
Rotunda, The
Sam's Grill
Savoy Brasserie
Schroeder's
Sears Fine Foods
Shadows, The
Silks
Splendido's
Square One
Squid's Cafe

Swan Oyster Depot
Tadich Grill
Tommy Toy's Chinoise
Trader Vic's
Tu Lan
Victor's
Yank Sing

East Bay

A la Carte
Augusta's
Bay Wolf
Betty's Ocean Diner
Bucci's
Cafe at Chez Panisse
Cafe De Bordeaux
Cafe Fanny
Caffe Venezia
California Cafe Bar & Grill
Carrera's
Casablanca
Chez Panisse
China Pavilion
China Station
Christopher's
Doug's BBQ
Edokko
Enoteca Mastro/S
Fat Apple's
Fourth Street Grill
Gertie's Chesapeake Bay
Gulf Coast Oyster Bar
Himalaya Restaurant
Jade Villa
Juan's Place
Kirala
Lalime's
La Mexicana
Lanzone Alexander
Le Marquis
Le Metropole
Long Life Vegi House
Mama's Royal Cafe
Middle East Restaurant
Mikado
Nadine's
Norman's Restaurant
Olivetto
Omnivore
Plearn Thai Cuisine
Riera's
Rue de Main
Santa Fe Bar/Grill
Saul's Delicatessen
Sedona Grill/Bar
Siam Cuisine
Spenger's Fish Grotto

Spiedini
Taiwan Restaurant
Thornhill Cafe
Ti Bacio
Tourelle
Triple Rock Brewery
Uncle Yu's
Via Veneto
Wine Bistro/Solano
Yoshi's Rest.
Yujean's
Zza's

Haight-Ashbury

Cha Cha Cha's

Japantown

Benihana
Korea House
Mifune
Sanppo
Seoul Garden

Marin

Adriana's
Alessia
Alta Mira Restaurant
Avenue Grill
Baci
Barnaby's By The Bay/N
Butler's
Cactus Cafe
Cairo Cafe
California Cafe Bar & Grill
Cantina, The
Caprice, The
Carlo's Restaurant
Casa Madrona
Chevys
Christophe
Citrus Grill
Dipsea Cafe
El Paseo
Feng Nian
Flynn's Landing
Giramonti
Goro's Robato
Gray Whale/N
Guaymas
Guernica
Horizons
Il Fornaio
Island Cafe
La Ginestra
La Petite Auberge

Lark Creek Inn, The
Lucca Ristorante
Mandarin House
Marin Joe's
Milly's
North Sea Village
Panama Hotel
Rice Table
Ristorante Fabrizio
Royal Thai
Sam's Anchor Cafe
Samui
Samurai
Sand Dollar/N
Savannah Grill

Mission

Bruno's
Cuba
Dusit Thai
El Tazumal
La Rondalla
La Taqueria
La Traviata
Le Domino
Le Trou Restaurant
Manora's Thai Cuisine
Nicaragua Restaurant
Original Old Clam Hse.
Roosevelt Tamale
Taqueria Mission

Nob Hill

Bella Voce
Fournou's Oven
French Room, The
Le Club
Lehr's Greenhouse
Nob Hill Restaurant
1001 Nob Hill Rest.
Squire Restaurant
Vanessi's

North Beach

Alfred's
Amelio's
Basta Pasta
Bohemian Cigar Store
Brandy Ho's
Brasserie Tomo
Buca Giovani
Cafe Greco
Caffe Roma
Caffe Sport
Capp's Corner

Fior d'Italia
I Fratelli
Little City Antipasti Bar
Little Joe's
New San Remo
North Beach Restaurant
Ristorante Grifone
Tommaso's
Trattoria Contadina
U.S. Restaurant
Washington Sq. Bar/Grill

Pacific Heights

Curbside Cafe
DePaula's Restaurant
El Drisco Hotel
Elite Cafe, The
Jackson Fillmore
Kim's
La Fiammetta Ristorante
La Mediterranee
La Rocca's Oyster Bar
Le Castel
Oritalia
Osome
Pacific Hts. Bar/Grill
Ploy Thai
Tortola Restaurant
Trio Cafe
Vivande Porta Via

Peninsula

Barrio Fiesta
Bella Vista
Brother's Delicatessen
Dal Baffo
Flea Street Cafe
Flower Lounge
Jin Jiang Kee Joon
Stanford Park
231 Ellsworth
Yuen Yung

Potrero Hill

Aux Delices
Flying Saucer
Il Pirata
Sally's
San Francisco BBQ
S. Asimakopoulous

Richmond

Acropolis Deli
Alejandro's Sociedad
Angkor Wat

Bill's Place
Cafe Riggio
Cambodia House
Cheer's Cafe
Chu Lin
Clement St. Bar/Grill
Cliff House
Courtyard, The
Ebisu
El Sombrero
Ernesto's
Fook, The
Fountain Court
Golden Turtle
Java Restaurant
Kabuto Sushi
Khan Toke Thai House
King Charcoal BBQ Hse.
King of China
Kirin
La Bergerie
Laghi
L'Avenue
Le Cyrano
Le St. Tropez
Mai's
Mamounia
Mandalay
Mel's Diner
Mescolanza
Mike's Chinese Cuisine
Milano Pizzeria
Miz Brown's Feed Bag
Narai
Ocean Restaurant
Pacific Cafe
Straits Cafe
Tanuki
Ton Kiang
Vegi Food
Yet Wah

Hamburger Mary's
Harpoon Louie's
Julie's Supper Club
Max's Diner
Milano Joe's
Roti
Ruby's
South Park Cafe
Umberto's
Undici
Wu Kong
Ya Ya's

Sunset

Cafe For All Seasons
Casa Aguila
Milano
Tien Fu

Union Street

Angkor Palace
Balboa Cafe
Bayon, The
Blue Light Cafe
Bonta
Brazen Head
Doidge's Kitchen
Franco's
Green's
Izzy's Steak/Chop Hse.
La Pergola
L'Entrecote de Paris
L'Escargot
Monroe's
North India Rest.
Parma
Perry's
Pietro's
Pixley Cafe
Prego Ristorante
Rodin
Ronayne's
Scott's Seafood Grill/S
Viareggio
Vlasta's European
Yoshida-Ya

SOMA

Ace Cafe
American Chow
Asta
Bricks
Cadillac Bar & Rest.
Caribbean Zone
City Block
Don Ramon's
Eddie Jacks
Eddie Rickenbacher's
Embarko
Etrusca
Fly Trap Restaurant

Van Ness/Polk

Acqurello
Adriatic
Cafe Majestic
Cordon Bleu Vietnamese
Emerald Garden
Golden Turtle
Hahn's Hibachi

Hard Rock Cafe
Harris' Restaurant
House of Prime Rib
La Folie
Little Henry's
Maye's Oyster House
Mekong
Pasha
Peacock, The
Phnom Penh
Swan Oyster Depot
Tommy's Joynt
Tutto Bene
Zola's

Wharf

Alioto's Restaurant
A. Sabella's
Castagnola's
El Tapatio
Gaylord Restaurant
Mandarin, The
Old Swiss House
Paprika's Fono
Scoma's
Tarantino Restaurant
Vicolo Pizzeria
Waterfront Restaurant
Yet Wah

BEYOND SAN FRANCISCO

North

Mendocino

Cafe Beaujolais

Napa

Auberge du Soleil
Brava Terrace
Domaine Chandon
French Laundry
Mustard's Grill
Piatti
Starmont
Terra

Tra Vigne
Trilogy
Vines

Sonoma

Chateau Souverain
Downtown Bakery
Grille, The
John Ash & Co.
Kenwood Restaurant
Madrona Manor
Station House Cafe

South

Half Moon Bay

San Benito House
Swedish Place

Los Altos

Beau Sejour
Chef Chu's

Monterey/Carmel

Abalonetti
Casanova
Central
Chaminade
Covey Restaurant
Crow's Nest
Fresh Cream
Giuliano's
Rio Grill
Sardine Factory

Mountain View

Chez T.J.

Palo Alto

California Cafe Bar & Grill
Chantilly Francais
L'Escale
Osteria

Redwood City

Baccarat Room
Barbarossa

Clark's by the Bay

San Jose

Adriatic Restaurant
Australian Restaurant
Alexander's
California Cafe Bar & Grill
Campbell House
El Maghreb
Emile's
Eulipia
Fung Lum
Gervais
J.R. Chops
La Foret
La Mere Michelle
Le Mouton Noir
Le Papillon
Les Saisons
L'Horizon Restaurant
Lion and Compass
Pacific Fresh (Sunnyvale)
Paolo's
Palermo
Plumed Horse, The
Sinaloa
Sue's Kitchen
Taco Al Pastor
Teske's Germania
Victorian Garden Rest.

Santa Cruz

Chaminade
Crow's Nest
Library, The

131

SPECIAL FEATURES AND APPEALS

Bar Scenes

Ace Cafe
Balboa Cafe
Bentley's
Big Four
Billboard Cafe
Bix
Cadillac Bar & Rest.
Cantina, The
Carnelian Room
Chevys
Clark's by the Bay/S
Clement St. Bar/Grill
Cliff House
Club Regent-Fairmont*
Corona Bar/Grill
Eddie Rickenbacher's
Elite Cafe, The
Embarko
Enrico's
Fior d'Italia
Flynn's Landing
Fog City Diner
Guaymas
Hamburger Mary's
Hard Rock Cafe
Izzy's Steak/Chop Hse.
Julie's Supper Club
Kimball's*
Kuleto's
Lark Creek Inn
L'Avenue
Le Central
Little City Antipasti Bar
London Wine Bar, The
MacArthur Park
Max's Opera Cafe
Miss Pearl's Jam House
Mustard's Grill/N
New Orleans-Fairmont*
North Beach Restaurant
Pacific Hts. Bar/Grill
Pat O'Shea's*
Perry's
Prego Ristorante
Postrio
Redwood Room* (Clift
  Hotel)
Rio Grill/S
Sam's Anchor Cafe
Sardine Factory/S
Sedona Grill/Bar
Southside*

Spiedini
Splendido's
Stars
Tommy's Joynt
Top of the Mark* (Mark
  Hopkins)
Trader Vic's
Tra Vigne/N
Triple Rock Brewery
Tutto Bene
Vanessi's
Victor's
Washington Sq. Bar/Grill
Waterfront Restaurant
Yoshi's Rest.
Zuni Cafe
(*Not in *Survey*)

Breakfast
(All major hotels
  and the following)

Acropolis Deli
Act IV
Alta Mira Restaurant
Bella Voce
Betty's Ocean Diner
Big Four
Bohemian Cigar Store
Brother's Delicatessen
Cafe Beaujolais/N
Cafe Claude
Cafe Fanny
Cafe Majestic
Cafe 222
Caffe Roma
Caffe Venezia
Campton Place
Casanova/S
Castagnola's
Celadon
Chambord
Chaminade/S
Cheer's Cafe
Cliff House
Curbside Cafe
Dipsea Cafe
Doidge's Kitchen
Donatello
El Drisco Hotel
Fat Apple's
Flea Street Cafe
Fook, The
French Room, The

132

Green's
Hamburger Mary's
Kuleto's
Lori's Diner
MacArthur Park
Madrona Manor/N
Mama's
Mama's Royal Cafe
Mekong
Mel's Diner
Miss Pearl's Jam House
Miz Brown's Feed Bag
Moishe's Pipick
Mom is Cooking
Nan Yang
New Joe's
1001 Nob Hill Rest.
Original Joe's
Pacific Grill
Park Grill
Ping Yuen
Postrio
Sally's
Saul's Delicatessen
Sears Fine Foods
Spenger's Fish Grotto
Spuntino
Stanford Park
Stars Cafe
Station House Cafe/N
Swedish Place/S
Taco Al Pastor/S
Trio Cafe
Zuni Cafe

Brunch

Alta Mira Restaurant
American Chow
A. Sabella's
Augusta's
Avenue Grill
Balboa Cafe
Barnaby's By The Bay/N
Basta Pasta
Bella Voce
Butler's
Cafe Beaujolais/N
Cafe De Bordeaux
Cafe For All Seasons
Cafe Majestic
Caffe Roma
Campton Place
Cantina, The
Casa Madrona
Clark's by the Bay/S
Cliff House
Courtyard, The

Diamond St. Rest.
El Drisco Hotel
Elite Cafe, The
Fat Apple's
Flea Street Cafe
Flower Lounge
Fook, The
French Room, The
Gaylord Restaurant
Gertie's Chesapeake Bay
Geva's
Grille, The
Green's
Hamburger Mary's
Horizons
Hyde St. Bistro
Il Fornaio
Island Cafe
John Ash & Co./N
Korea House
Kuleto's
Lark Creek Inn
L'Avenue
L'Entrecote de Paris
Leticia's
Lori's Diner
MacArthur Park
Madrona Manor/N
Mama's
Mama's Royal Cafe
Mandarin, The
Mekong
Mel's Diner
Miss Pearl's Jam House
Miz Brown's Feed Bag
Nan Yang
Narsai's Cafe
Norman's Restaurant
North Beach Restaurant
North India Rest.
Ocean Restaurant
Old Swiss House
Original Joe's
Pacific Fresh
Pacific Hts. Bar/Grill
Pacific Grill
Paprika's Fono
Park Grill
Perry's
Pierre at Meridien
Pier 23 Cafe
Ping Yuen
Pixley Cafe
Postrio
Prego Ristorante
Regina's
Riera's

Rio Grill/S
Ronayne's
Sally's
Sam's Anchor Cafe
Sand Dollar/N
Santa Fe Bar/Grill
Saul's Delicatessen
Savannah Grill
Scott's Seafood Grill/S
Sears Fine Foods
Silks
Spenger's Fish Grotto
Spuntino
Stanford Park
Starmont/N
Stars Cafe
Station House Cafe/N
Swedish Place/S
Taco Al Pastor/S
Taiwan Restaurant
Ti Bacio
Tortola Restaurant
Tourelle
Trio Cafe
Tung Fong
Victorian Garden Rest./S
Victor's
Washington Sq. Bar/Grill
Waterfront Restaurant
Zuni Cafe

Business Meetings

Acqurello
Adriatic
Adriatic Restaurant
Alexander's/S
Alioto's Restaurant
Alta Mira Restaurant
Asta
Auberge du Soleil/N
Barnaby's By The Bay/N
Benihana
Big Four
Bix
Brava Terrace/N
Bruno's
Bucci's
Butler's
Cafe Beaujolais/N
Cafe De Bordeaux
Cafe Majestic
Caffe Roma
California Cafe Bar & Grill
Calif. Culinary Academy
Campton Place
Caprice, The

Caribbean Zone
Carnelian Room
Casa Madrona
Celadon
Chambord
Chantilly Francais/S
Chateau Souverain/N
Citrus Grill
Crow's Nest/S
Dal Baffo
Donatello
Don Ramon's
Ebisu
El Drisco Hotel
Empress of China
Enoteca Lanzone
Ernie's
Etrusca
Faz Restaurant/Bar
Feng Nian
565 Clay
Flower Lounge
Fournou's Oven
French Room, The
Gertie's Chesapeake Bay
Gervais/S
Green's
Grille, The
Harris' Restaurant
House of Prime Rib
Hunan Restaurant
Iron Horse, The
Jack's
Jade Villa
John Ash & Co./N
Julius' Castle
Kansai
Korea House
La Mediterranee
La Mere Duquesne
Lark Creek Inn, The
La Rondalla
Le Central
Le Marquis
L'Entrecote de Paris
Le Papillon/S
Little Italy
L'Olivier
Los Chiles
MacArthur Park
Madrona Manor/N
Mai's
Mamounia
Mandarin House
Mela
Milly's
Monsoon

Mustard's Grill/N
New Joe's
New San Remo
Nob Hill Restaurant
North Beach Restaurant
North India Rest.
Old Swiss House
1001 Nob Hill Rest.
Osome
Pacific Hts. Bar/Grill
Paolo's/S
Pasha
Pierre at Meridien
Postrio
Regina's
Ristorante Fabrizio
Rosalie's
Rotunda, The
Ruth's Chris Steakhouse*
Sardine Factory/S
Saul's Delicatessen
Schroeder's
Scott's Seafood Grill/S
Seoul Garden
Shadows, The
Silks
Spenger's Fish Grotto
Splendido's
Squid's Cafe
Square One
Squire Restaurant
Stars
Ton Kiang
Tourelle
Trader Vic's
Trattoria Contadina
Tra Vigne/N
Umberto's
Uncle Yu's
Vanessi's
Via Veneto
Victor's
Yamato Sukiyaki Hse.
Yoshi's Rest.
Zola's
(*Not in *Survey*)

Caters

Acqurello
Acropolis Deli
Act IV
Adriatic Restaurant
A la Carte
Alta Mira Restaurant
Auberge du Soleil/N
Augusta's

Australian Restaurant/S
Avenue Grill
Barnaby's By The Bay/N
Beau Sejour/S
Bella Voce
Betty's Ocean Diner
Bill's Place
Bix
Brava Terrace/N
Brother's Delicatessen
Cafe Claude
Cafe Fanny
Cantina, The
Celadon
Chambord
Chaminade/S
Cheer's Cafe
Chef Chu's/S
Chevys
China Pavilion
Cliff House
Donatello
Doug's BBQ
Downtown Bakery/N
Ebisu
Etrusca
Eulipia/S
Flea Street Cafe
Fook, The
Fournou's Oven
French Room, The
Fung Lum/S
Gaylord Restaurant
Gertie's Chesapeake Bay
Gervais/S
Geva's
Goro's Robato
Hahn's Hibachi
Hyde St. Bistro
India House
Iron Horse, The
Jade Villa
Java Restaurant
Kansai
Kim's
King Charcoal BBQ Hse.
Korea House
La Mediterranee
La Mexicana
La Petite Auberge
Lascaux
Lehr's Greenhouse
Leticia's
Long Life Vegi House
Lori's Diner
MacArthur Park
Mela

Miss Pearl's Jam House
Moishe's Pipick
Monsoon
Nob Hill Restaurant
Ocean City
Osome
Pacific Grill
Panama Hotel
Paolo's/S
Park Grill
Pasha
Phnom Penh
Pier 23 Cafe
Prego Ristorante
Regina's
Riera's
Rotunda, The
Ruby's
Sally's
San Francisco BBQ
S. Asimakopoulous
Saul's Delicatessen
Savannah Grill
Schroeder's
Sedona Grill/Bar
Seoul Garden
Siam Cuisine
Silks
Spenger's Fish Grotto
Squid's Cafe
Stanford Park
Straits Cafe
Sue's Kitchen/S
Swedish Place/S
Taco Al Pastor/S
Tanuki
Tarantino's Restaurant
Tien Fu
Trader Vic's
Tra Vigne/N
Tutto Bene
Umberto's
Uncle Yu's
Viareggio
Victorian Garden Rest./S
Vivande Porta Via
Washington Sq. Bar/Grill
Yamato Sukiyaki Hse.
Yet Wah
Yoshi's Rest.
Yuen Yung

Dancing
(Check days and times)

Avenue Ballroom* (swing)
Caesar's Latin Palace*
  (Latin)
Cal's* (rock)
Das Klub* (rock)
Dreamland* (disco)
DV8 Club* (rock)
Great Amer. Music Hall*
  (rock)
I-Beam* (rock)
Juke Box Sat. Night*
  (rock)
New Orleans* (Dixieland)
Oasis* (rock)
Oz* (pop)
Paradise Lounge (disco)
Rockin' Robins* (rock)
Slim's* (rock)
Southside* (rock)
Tonga* (ballroom)
Tracadero Transfer*
  (disco)
Warfield, The* (rock)
(*Not in *Survey*)

Delivers
(Among the many)

Acropolis Deli
Betty's Ocean Diner
Cafe Fanny
Chambord
DePaula's Restaurant
Hahn's Hibachi
I Fratelli
Jade Villa
Kansai
Little Henry's
Milano Pizzeria
Moishe's Pipick
Osome
Pier 23 Cafe
Ruby's
Shroeder's
Uncle Yu's
Vivande Porta Via
Yoshi's Rest.

Dessert (D) and Ice Cream (I)
(Besides Baskin Robbins)

Bud's Ice Cream* (I)
Double Rainbow* (I)
Downtown Bakery/N (D, I)
Fantasia* (D)
Gelato Classico* (I)
Joe's Ice Cream* (I)
Just Desserts (D)
La Nouvelle Patisserie* (D)

Mary's* (D)
Rory's Twisted Scoop* (I)
SF Desserts* (D)
Sweet Inspiration* (D)
Swensens* (I)
Toy Boat Dessert Cafe* (D)
True Confections* (D)
Uncle Gaylord's* (I)
(*Not in *Survey*)

Dining Alone
(Other than hotels)

Ace Cafe
Act IV
Avenue Grill
Basta Pasta
Benihana
Bentley's
Betty's Ocean Diner
Bill's Place
Bohemian Cigar Store
Cafe at Chez Panisse
Casa Aguila
China Moon Cafe
Doidge's Kitchen
Doug's BBQ
Ebisu
Elite Cafe, The
Flynn's Landing
Fog City Diner
Hamburger Mary's
Hard Rock Cafe
Hog Heaven*
Isobune Sushi
Jackson Fillmore
Kabuto Sushi
Lark Creek Inn
La Taqueria
MacArthur Park
Max's Diner
Max's Opera Cafe
Miz Brown's Feed Bag
Mom is Cooking
Osome
Pacific Hts. Bar/Grill
Perry's
Sam's Anchor Cafe
Sanppo
Schroeder's
Spuntino
Stars
Stars Cafe
Swan Oyster Depot
Tadich Grill
Tommy's Joynt
Yoshida-Ya
Zza's
(*Not in *Survey*)

Entertainment
(Check days and times;
  complete listing in
  Sunday newspapers)

Angkor Wat (belly dancing)
Auberge du Sol./N (piano)
Beethoven (piano)
Bentley's (piano)
Big Four (piano)
Cafe Majestic (piano)
Casablanca (piano)
Chambord (piano)
Circolo (piano)
El Maghreb/S (folk music)
El Tapatio (folk music)
Etrusca (piano)
Fournou's Oven (piano)
French Room (piano)
Harris' Restaurant (piano)
Lafayette on Pac. (piano)
Lascaux (piano)
L'Entrecote (piano)
Maltese Grill (piano)
Mandarin House (piano)
Marrakech (belly dancers)
Max's Cafe (piano)
Nob Hill Rest. (piano)
Pacific Grill (piano)
Pasha (jazz)
Pier 23 Cafe (jazz)
Plumed Horse, The/S (piano)
Regina's (piano)
Santa Fe Bar/Grill (piano)
Silks (piano)
Starmont/N (piano)
Stars (piano)
Station Hse. Cafe/N (piano)
Via Veneto (piano)
Washington Sq. Bar (jazz)

Fireplaces

Act IV
A la Carte
Amelio's
Auberge du Soleil/N
Bella Vista
Bentley's
Big Four
Brava Terrace/N
Cafe Beaujolais/N
Cafe Mozart
Campbell House
Caprice, The
Chambord
Chantilly Francais/S
Clement St. Bar/Grill
Cliff House

Covey Restaurant/S
El Paseo
El Tapatio
French Laundry/N
Fresh Cream/S
Goro's Robato
Guaymas
Horizons
House of Prime Rib
Izzy's Steak/Chop Hse.
John Ash & Co./N
Lalime's
Lark Creek Inn
Lascaux
Le Metropole
Le Mouton Noir/S
Le St. Tropez
Los Chiles
Madrona Manor/N
Mandarin House
Marin Joe's
Monsoon
Old Swiss House
1001 Nob Hill Rest.
Pacific Grill
Plumed Horse, The/S
Rio Grill/S
Sand Dollar/N
Sardine Factory/S
Sharl's*
Stanford Park
Starmont/N
Swedish Place/S
Tourelle
Zuni Cafe
(*Not in *Survey*)

Game in Season
(Order in advance)

Acqurello
Bix
Caribbean Zone
Ernie's
Hyde St. Bistro
I Fratelli
Iron Horse, The
Lark Creek Inn
Mela
1001 Nob Hill Rest.
Squire Restaurant
Starmont/N
Stars
Tourelle

Garden and Outdoor Dining

Adriana's
Adriatic Restaurant

Alessia
Alta Mira Restaurant
Auberge du Soleil/N
Augusta's
Australian Restaurant/S
Barnaby's By The Bay/N
Bay Wolf
Bill's Place
Brava Terrace/N
Bucci's
Butler's
Cafe Beaujolais/N
Cafe Claude
Cafe Fanny
Caffe Roma
Cantina, The
Carlo's Restaurant
Casanova/S
Chambord
Chaminade/S
Chateau Souverain/N
Cheer's Cafe
Chevys
Citrus Grill
Crow's Nest/S
Domaine Chandon/N
El Tapatio
Emerald Garden
French Laundry/N
Gertie's Chesapeake Bay
Geva's
Gray Whale/N
Guaymas
Horizons
Il Fornaio
John Ash & Co./N
Kenwood Restaurant/N
Khan Toke Thai House
La Mere Michelle/S
Lark Creek Inn
L'Entrecote de Paris
L'Horizon Restaurant/S
Little Joe's
MacArthur Park
Madrona Manor/N
Marin Joe's
Miss Pearl's Jam House
Mustard's Grill/N
Original Old Clam Hse.
Panama Hotel
Pasta Moon
Perry's
Pier 23 Cafe
Rio Grill/S
Sam's Anchor Cafe
San Benito House/S
Sardine Factory/S
Savannah Grill
Stanford Park
Starmont/N

Teske's Germania/S
Thornhill Cafe
Tourelle
Tra Vigne/N
Trio Cafe
Vicolo Pizzeria
Victorian Garden Rest./S
Vines/N
Yamato Sukiyaki Hse.
Zuni Cafe
(*Not in *Survey*)

Health/Spa Menus

Covey Restaurant/S
565 Clay
French Room, The
Green's
Grille, The
Hard Rock Cafe
Island Cafe
Julie's Supper Club
Julius' Castle
La Mediterranee
La Rocca's Oyster Bar
Long Life Vegi House
Pacific Fresh
Spuntino
Starmont/N
Stars
Trio Cafe
Washington Sq. Bar/Grill

Historic Interest

1930 Alfred's
1927 Alioto's
1926 Amelio's
1850 Cliff House
1886 Fior d'Italia
1933 French Room, The
1946 House of Prime Rib
1950 Iron Horse, The
1864 Jack's
1938 Original Joe's
1861 Original Old Clam Hse.
1867 Sam's Grill
1893 Schroeder's
1940 Sear's Fine Foods
1890 Spenger's
1849 Tadich Grill
1949 Tommy's Joynt
1951 Trader Vic's

Hotel Dining

Alta Mira Hotel
  Alta Mira Restaurant
Auberge du Soleil
  Auberge du Soleil/N

Campton Place
  Campton Place
Donatello Hotel
  Donatello
El Drisco Hotel
  El Drisco Hotel
Fairmont Hotel – SF
  Bella Voce
  Mason's
  Squire, The
Fairmont Hotel – San Jose
  Les Saisons/S
Four Seasons Clift Hotel
  French Room, The
Galleria Park
  Bentley's
Garden Court Hotel
  Il Fornaio
Hotel Griffon
  Roti
Hotel Nikko
  Cafe 222
Hotel Sofitel
  Baccarat Room/S
Huntington Hotel
  Big Four
  L'Etoile
Hyatt Regency
  Equinox*
Hyatt Union Square
  One Up*
Inn at the Opera
  Act IV
Julianna Hotel
  Palm, The
Madrona Manor Inn
  Madrona Manor/N
Majestic Hotel
  Cafe Majestic
Mandarin Hotel
  Silks
Mark Hopkins Hotel
  Nob Hill Restaurant
Marriott Hotel
  Alexander's/S
Meadowood Resort
  Starmont/N
Meridien
  Pierre at Meridien
Park Hyatt Hotel
  Park Grill
Panama Hotel
  Panama Rest.
Pan Pacific Hotel
  Pacific Grill
Phoenix Inn
  Miss Pearl's Jam House
Portman Hotel
  Portman Grill

Prescott Hotel
  Postrio
Quail Lodge, The
  Covey Restaurant/S
Regis Hotel
  Regina's
Shannon Hotel
  La Mere Duquesne
Shattuck Hotel
  Sedona Grill/Bar
Sonoma Mission Inn
  Grille, The
St. Francis Hotel
  Victor's
Stanford Court Hotel
  Fournou's Oven
Stanford Park Hotel
  Stanford Park
Villa Florence Hotel
  Kuleto's
Vintage Court
  Masa's
(*Not in *Survey*)

"In" Places

Ace Cafe
Acqurello
Amelio's
Auberge du Soleil/N
Balboa Cafe
Barnaby's By The Bay/N
Bay Wolf
Bentley's
Bix
Blue Light Cafe
Brava Terrace/N
Butler's
Cadillac Bar & Rest.
Cafe at Chez Panisse
Cafe Riggio
Caffe Sport
Cambodia House
Campton Place
Central/S
Chez Panisse
China Moon Cafe
Circolo
Crow's Nest/S
Donatello
Eddie Jacks
Elite Cafe, The
Enoteca Lanzone
Enoteca Mastro/S
Ernie's
Fat Apple's
Fleur de Lys
Flower Lounge

Fog City Diner
Fourth Street Grill
French Room, The
Fresh Cream/S
Gertie's Chesapeake Bay
Green's
Guaymas
Hamburger Mary's
Harbor Village
Hard Rock Cafe
Harris' Restaurant
Hayes Street Grill
Janot's
John Ash & Co./N
Julie's Supper Club
Lalime's
L'Avenue
Le Central
Le Club
Little City Antipasti Bar
MacArthur Park
Masa's
Max's Diner
Miss Pearl's Jam House
Mustard's Grill/N
1001 Nob Hill Rest.
Osteria
Pacific Cafe
Perry's
Pierre at Meridien
Pier 23 Cafe
Plearn Thai Cuisine
Prego Ristorante
Rio Grill/S
Savoy Brasserie
Sedona Grill/Bar
Spuntino
Squid's Cafe
Starmont/N
Stars
Swan Oyster Depot
Tadich Grill
Thep Phanom
Tommaso's
Tourelle
Trader Vic's
Tra Vigne/N
231 Ellsworth
Undici
Washington Sq. Bar/Grill
Zuni Cafe

Jacket Required

Amelio's
Auberge du Soleil/N
Baccarat Room/S
Beau Sejour/S

Big Four
Cafe Majestic
Carnelian Room
Celadon
Covey Restaurant/S
Domaine Chandon/N
Donatello
El Drisco Hotel
Empress of China
Enoteca Lanzone
Ernie's
Fior d'Italia
French Room, The
Harris' Restaurant
Imperial Palace
India House
Jack's
Janot's
Jin Jiang Kee Joon
Julius' Castle
Le Club
Le St. Tropez
Monroe's
Nob Hill Restaurant
Paolo's/S
Peacock, The
Pierre at Meridien
Shadows, The
Silks
Squire Restaurant
Starmont/N
Trader Vic's
Victor's

Late Late –
After Midnight

(All hours are AM;
check weekday times
which may be earlier)

Ace Cafe (12)
Alejandro's Sociedad (12)
Balboa Cafe (12)
Basta Pasta (1:30)
Bohemian Cigar Store (1)
Brazen Head (12:45)
Bruno's (2)
Cadillac Bar (12)
Caffe Roma (1)
Cliff House (12)
Fog City Diner (12)
Hamburger Mary's (1:30)
Hard Rock Cafe (12)
Imperial Palace (2)
Kabuto Sushi (2)
Korea House (3)
La Rondalla (3:30)
Le Piano Zinc (12)

Little City Bar (12)
Mama's (3:30)
Marin Joe's (12:45)
Max's Diner (1)
Max's Opera Cafe (1)
Original Joe's (1:30)
Pasha (12)
Perry's (12)
Siam Cuisine (12)
Spuntino (1)
Taiwan Rest. (2)
Tien Fu (2:30)
Trader Vic's (12:30)
Yoshi's Rest. (12)
Yuet Lee (3)

Noteworthy
Closings

Billboard Cafe
Daniel's
Da Sandro
Doro's
Enrico's
Four Star Rest.
Harry's Bar & Amer. Grill
Jil's
Knickerbockers
L'Etoile
Max's Deli
Maxwell's
Miramonte
Mitoya
Palm, The
Peacock, The
Premier Cru Cafe
Post St. Bar & Grill
Raf
Rosalie's
Shelly's Italian
Sobel Cafe
Sushi Gen
Taxi
Waverly Place

Noteworthy
Newcomers

Asta
Brava Terrace/N
Cafe Claude
Cafe De Bordeaux
Cafe Greco
Cairo Cafe
Caribbean Zone
Casablanca
Central
Cha Cha Cha's

Chantilly Francais/S
Citrus Grill
Embarko
Enoteca Lanzone
Enoteca Mastro/S
Etrusca
Flying Saucer
Hyde St. Bistro
La Bergerie
Laghi
Lanzone Alexander
Mela
Monsoon
Nan Yang
Pacific Grill
Park Grill
Ruby's
Savoy Brasserie
Splendido's
Undici
Ya Ya's

Noteworthy Yearlings

Acqurello
Act IV
Butler's
Cafe 222
Casa Aguila
Chateau Souverain/N
City Block
Eddie Jacks
House of Nanking
Kirala
La Folie
Lark Creek Inn
Mirabelle
Moishe's Pipick
North Sea Village
1001 Nob Hill Rest.
Oritalia
Pacific Grill
Palermo/S
Piatti/N
Postrio
Roti
Samui
Saul's Delicatessen
690
South Park Cafe
Starmont/N
Terra/N
Thep Phanom
Tortola Restaurant
Tourelle
Trilogy/N

Wu Kong
Yujean's
Zza's

Offbeat

Acropolis Deli
American Chow
Bella Voce
Brother's Delicatessen
Cadillac Bar & Rest.
Cafe at Chez Panisse
Caffe Sport
Calif. Culinary Academy
Caribbean Zone
Cha Cha Cha's
Crow's Nest/S
Eddie Jacks
Fat Apple's
Fog City Diner
Gertie's Chesapeake Bay
Geva's
Green's
Hamburger Mary's
Hard Rock Cafe
Julie's Supper Club
La Rondalla
Little City Antipasti Bar
Max's Diner
Max's Opera Cafe
Mela
Miss Pearl's Jam House
Pasha
Pier 23 Cafe
Plearn Thai Cuisine
S. Asimakopoulous
Seoul Garden
Squid's Cafe
Thep Phanom
Trader Vic's
Yoshi's Rest.

Parties
(See also Private Rooms)

Abalonetti/S
A la Carte
Alejandro's Sociedad
Alexander's/S
Alfred's
Alioto's Restaurant
Alta Mira Restaurant
A. Sabella's
Asta
Auberge du Soleil/N
Barbarossa/S
Blue Fox, The
Bruno's

Cafe Majestic
Cafe Mozart
California Cafe Bar & Grill
Calif. Culinary Academy
Cambodia House
Campton Place
Caprice, The
Caribbean Zone
Carnelian Room
Casa Madrona
Celadon
Chambord
Chantilly Francais/S
Chateau Souverain/N
China Pavilion
Chu Lin
Citrus Grill
Covey Restaurant/S
Dal Baffo
Donatello
Don Ramon's
Ebisu
El Drisco Hotel
Empress of China
Enoteca Lanzone
Ernie's
Faz Restaurant/Bar
Fior d'Italia
Flower Lounge
Fournou's Oven
French Laundry/N
French Room, The
Gaylord Restaurant
Gervais/S
Guaymas
Guernica
Harris' Restaurant
Hunan Restaurant
Imperial Palace
Iron Horse, The
Jack's
John Ash & Co./N
Julius' Castle
Kabuto Sushi
Kansai
Korea House
Lalime's
La Mere Duquesne
Lark Creek Inn
L'Avenue
Le Metropole
L'Entrecote de Paris
Le Papillon/S
Les Saisons/S
Little Italy
L'Olivier
Long Life Vegi House
Los Chiles

Lucca Ristorante
MacArthur Park
Madrona Manor/N
Mai's
Mamounia
Mandarin House
Marin Joe's
Mela
Miss Pearl's Jam House
Monsoon
Nadine's
New Joe's
New San Remo
Nob Hill Restaurant
North Beach Restaurant
North India Rest.
Ocean Restaurant
Old Swiss House
1001 Nob Hill Rest.
Osome
Pacific Hts. Bar/Grill
Paolo's/S
Pasha
Pierre at Meridien
Postrio
Regina's
Sam's Grill
Samurai
Sardine Factory/S
Schroeder's
Scoma's
Seoul Garden
Shadows, The
Silks
690
Spenger's Fish Grotto
Square One
Squid's Cafe
Squires Restaurant, The
Starmont/N
Stars
Tourelle
Trader Vic's
Trattoria Contadina
Tra Vigne/N
Umberto's
Vanessi's
Via Veneto
Vlasta's European
Yet Wah
Yoshida-Ya
Yoshi's Rest.

Private Rooms
(Also all major hotels)

Abalonetti/S
A la Carte

Alejandro's Sociedad
Alexander's/S
Alfred's
Alioto's Restaurant
Alta Mira Restaurant
Asta
A. Sabella's
Auberge du Soleil/N
Barbarossa/S
Blue Fox, The
Bruno's
Cafe Majestic
Cafe Mozart
California Cafe Bar & Grill
Calif. Culinary Academy
Cambodia House
Campton Place
Caprice, The
Caribbean Zone
Carnelian Room
Casa Madrona
Celadon
Chambord
Chantilly Francais/S
Chateau Souverain/N
China Pavilion
Chu Lin
Citrus Grill
Covey Restaurant/S
Dal Baffo
Donatello
Don Ramon's
Ebisu
El Drisco Hotel
Empress of China
Enoteca Lanzone
Ernie's
Faz Restaurant/Bar
Fior d'Italia
Flower Lounge
Fournou's Oven
French Laundry/N
French Room, The
Gaylord Restaurant
Gervais/S
Guaymas
Guernica
Harris' Restaurant
Hunan Restaurant
Imperial Palace
Iron Horse, The
Jack's
John Ash & Co./N
Julius' Castle
Kabuto Sushi
Kansai
Korea House
Lalime's

La Mere Duquesne
Lark Creek Inn
L'Avenue
Le Metropole
L'Entrecote de Paris
Le Papillon/S
Les Saisons/S
Little Italy
L'Olivier
Long Life Vegi House
Los Chiles
Lucca Ristorante
MacArthur Park
Madrona Manor/N
Mai's
Mamounia
Mandarin House
Marin Joe's
Mela
Miss Pearl's Jam House
Monsoon
Nadine's
New Joe's
New San Remo
Nob Hill Restaurant
North Beach Restaurant
North India Rest.
Ocean Restaurant
Old Swiss House
1001 Nob Hill Rest.
Osome
Pacific Hts. Bar/Grill
Paolo's/S
Paprika's Fono
Pasha
Pierre at Meridien
Postrio
Regina's
Sam's Grill
Samurai
Sardine Factory/S
Schroeder's
Seoul Garden
Shadows, The
Silks
690
Spenger's Fish Grotto
Square One
Squid's Cafe
Squire Restaurant
Starmont/N
Stars
Tourelle
Trader Vic's
Trattoria Contadina
Tra Vigne/N
Umberto's
Vanessi's

Vlasta's European
Yamato Sukiyaki Hse.
Yet Wah
Yoshida-Ya
Yoshi's Rest.
(*Not in *Survey*)

People-Watching

Balboa Cafe
Bentley's
Bix
Blue Fox, The
Eddie Rickenbacher's
Elite Cafe, The
Fog City Diner
Guaymas
Hard Rock Cafe
Kuleto's
Lark Creek Inn
L'Avenue
Le Central
Mustard's Grill/N
Pacific Hts. Bar/Grill
Perry's
Postrio
Prego Ristorante
Savoy Brasserie
Southside*
Square One
Stars
Trader Vic's
Tra Vigne/N
231 Ellsworth
Undici
Washington Sq. Bar/Grill
Zuni Cafe
(*Not in *Survey*)

Power Scenes

Amelio's
Big Four
Bix
Blue Fox, The
Campton Place
Donatello
French Room, The
Lark Creek Inn
Le Central
Masa's
Pacific Grill
Park Grill
Postrio
Sam's Grill
Sardine Factory/S
Square One
Stars
Tadich Grill

Trader Vic's
Vanessi's
Washington Sq. Bar/Grill

Prix Fixe Menus
(Call to check
 prices and times)

Abalonetti/S
Adriana's
Adriatic Restaurant
Alexander's/S
Alta Mira Restaurant
Auberge du Soleil/N
Barbarossa/S
Brasserie Tomo
Cafe at Chez Panisse
Cafe Mozart
Calif. Culinary Academy
Carnelian Room
Celadon
Chez Panisse
Circolo
Crow's Nest/S
Diamond St. Rest.
Donatello
Ebisu
Ernie's
Hunan Restaurant
India House
Jack's
Lalime's
Le Papillon/S
Le Piano Zinc
Madrona Manor/N
Mamounia
Masa's
Mela
Monsoon
New San Remo
North Beach Restaurant
North India Rest.
Park Grill
Pasha
Pierre at Meridien
Rodin
Samurai
San Francisco BBQ
Schroeder's
Scott's Seafood Grill/S
Seoul Garden
Shadows, The
Squire Restaurant
Starmont/N
Umberto's
Vanessi's
Victor's
Yamato Sukiyaki Hse.
Yujean's

Pubs

Clement St. Bar/Grill
Eddie Rickenbacher's
Edinburgh Castle*
Liverpool Lil's*
London Wine Bar, The
Pat O'Shea's*
Perry's
Tommy's Joynt
Washington Sq. Bar/Grill
(*Not in *Survey*)

Reservations Essential

Acqurello
Amelio's
Auberge du Soleil/N
Baccarat Room/S
Bayon, The
Bay Wolf
Bella Vista
Bix
Buca Giovani
Cadillac Bar & Rest.
Caffe Sport
Calif. Culinary Academy
Campton Place
Caprice, The
Carlo's Restaurant
Castagnola's
Chaminade/S
Chateau Souverain/N
Chez Panisse
Chez T.J./S
China Moon Cafe
China Pavilion
Domaine Chandon/N
Donatello
Eddie Jacks
Eddie Rickenbacher's
El Drisco Hotel
El Paseo
Embarko
Enoteca Lanzone
Ernie's
Etrusca
Flea Street Cafe
Fleur de Lys
Flower Lounge
Fog City Diner
French Laundry/N
French Room, The
Fresh Cream/S
Green's
Grille, The
Guaymas
Gulf Coast Oyster Bar
Hayes Street Grill

House of Nanking
Il Fornaio
Ivy's
Jack's
Janot's
John Ash & Co./N
Julius' Castle
Khan Toke Thai House
Kuleto's
La Folie
La Foret/S
Laghi
Lalime's
La Mere Michelle/S
La Petite Auberge
Lascaux
L'Avenue
Le Castel
Le Central
Le Club
Le Domino
Le Marquis
Le Metropole
Le Mouton Noir/S
Masa's
Monroe's
Monsoon
Mustard's Grill/N
Nan Yang
North Beach Restaurant
Omnivore
Osteria
Pacific Grill
Park Grill
Paolo's/S
Parma
Pasha
Perry's
Pier 23 Cafe
Pacific Grill
Postrio
Prego Ristorante
San Benito House/S
Santa Fe Bar/Grill
Scoma's
Silks
690
Square One
Squire Restaurant
Starmont/N
Stars
Tadich Grill
Terra/N
Thornhill Cafe
Tommy Toy's Chinoise
Trader Vic's
Tra Vigne/N
Trilogy/N

Tutto Bene
231 Ellsworth
Washington Sq. Bar/Grill
Wu Kong
Yoshida-Ya
Yoshi's Rest.
Yujean's
Zola's
Zuni Cafe

Romantic Spots

Acqurello
Adriatic Restaurant
Alexander's/S
Alta Mira Restaurant
Amelio's
Asta
Auberge du Soleil/N
Barbarossa/S
Barnaby's By The Bay/N
Bay Wolf
Bella Vista
Bentley's
Bix
Blue Fox, The
Blue Light Cafe
Brazen Head
Cafe at Chez Panisse
Cafe Beaujolais/N
Cafe Majestic
Cafe Mozart
Campton Place
Caprice, The
Carnelian Room
Casa Madrona
Chateau Souverain/N
Chez Panisse
Chez T.J./S
Christophe
Circolo
Domaine Chandon/N
Donatello
Eddie Jacks
El Drisco Hotel
Elite Cafe, The
El Paseo
Embarko
Enoteca Lanzone
Ernie's
Etrusca
Fior d'Italia
Fleur de Lys
Fournou's Oven
French Laundry/N
French Room, The
Gaylord Restaurant
Gertie's Chesapeake Bay

Green's
Grille, The
Harris' Restaurant
India House
Janot's
John Ash & Co./N
Julius' Castle
Kim's
La Folie
Lark Creek Inn
Le Castel
Le Club
L'Entrecote de Paris
Le Piano Zinc
Madrona Manor/N
Masa's
Mirabelle
Mustard's Grill/N
1001 Nob Hill Rest.
Paolo's/S
Park Grill
Pierre at Meridien
Pier 23 Cafe
Plearn Thai Cuisine
Postrio
Prego Ristorante
Silks
Square One
Squire Restaurant
Starmont/N
Stars
Tourelle
Tra Vigne/N
Trilogy/N
231 Ellsworth
Victor's
Waterfront Restaurant
Wu Kong
Zuni Cafe

Sidewalk Dining

Auberge du Soleil/N
Cafe Fanny
Caffe Roma
Cheer's Cafe
Circolo
Harbor Village
Hyde St. Bistro
L'Entrecote de Paris
Schroeder's
Zuni Cafe

Singles Scenes

Ace Cafe
Balboa Cafe
Billboard Cafe
Bohemian Cigar Store

Cadillac Bar & Rest.
Cafe Riggio
Cafe Sport
Caribbean Zone
Cha Cha Cha's
Chevys
Clark's by the Bay/S
Elite Cafe, The
Fog City Diner
Hamburger Mary's
Hard Rock Cafe
Lark Creek Inn
London Wine Bar, The
MacArthur Park
Miss Pearl's Jam House
Pacific Hts. Bar/Grill
Pat O'Shea's*
Perry's
Prego Ristorante
Rosalie's
Sam's Anchor Cafe
Savoy Brasserie
Scott's Seafood Grill/S
Southside*
Spuntino
Tutto Bene
Undici
Washington Sq. Bar/Grill
Zuni Cafe
(*Not in *Survey*)

Takeout
(Among others)

Abalonetti/S
Ace Cafe
Acropolis Deli
Adriatic
Alejandro's Sociedad
American Chow
Angkor Palace
Angkor Wat
Augusta's
Australian Restaurant/S
Aux Delices
Avenue Grill
Baci
Barnaby's By The Bay/N
Barrio Fiesta
Basta Pasta
Bayon, The
Benihana
Bill's Place
Blue Light Cafe
Bricks
Brother's Delicatessen
Bruno's
Butler's

Cactus Cafe
Cadillac Bar & Rest.
Cafe Beaujolais/N
Cafe Claude
Cafe De Bordeaux
Cafe Fanny
Caffe Roma
Caffe Sport
California Cafe Bar & Grill
Calif. Culinary Academy
Cambodia House
Cantina, The
Caribbean Zone
Casa Madrona
Casanova/S
Celadon
Chambord
Cheer's Cafe
Chef Chu's/S
Chevys
China Moon Cafe
China Pavilion
China Station
Christophe
Chu Lin
Citrus Grill
Cliff House
Cordon Bleu Vietnamese
Courtyard, The
Cuba
Curbside Cafe
DePaula's Restaurant
Diamond St. Rest.
Dipsea Cafe
Don Ramon's
Downtown Bakery/N
Ebisu
Edokko
El Sombrero
El Tapatio
El Tazumal
Emerald Garden
Ernesto's
Fat Apple's
Feng Nian
Flower Lounge
Flynn's Landing
Fook, The
Fourth Street Grill
French Room, The
Fung Lum/S
Gaylord Restaurant
Gertie's Chesapeake Bay
Golden Phoenix
Golden Turtle
Goro's Robato
Gray Whale/N
Green's

Gulf Coast Oyster Bar
Hahn's Hibachi
Hamburger Mary's
Harbor Village
Hard Rock Cafe
Hong Kong Tea House
Hunan Restaurant
Hyde St. Bistro
Il Fornaio
Il Pirata
Imperial Palace
India House
Indian Oven
Iron Horse, The
Isobune Sushi
Jade Villa
Java Restaurant
Jin Jiang Kee Joon
Juan's Place
Julie's Supper Club
Kabuto Sushi
Kansai
Kenwood Restaurant/N
Khan Toke Thai House
Kim's
King Charcoal BBQ Hse.
King of China
Kirala
Kirin
Korea House
La Ginestra
Lalime's
La Mediterranee
La Mexicana
La Rocca's Oyster Bar
La Rondalla
La Taqueria
Lehr's Greenhouse
L'Escale/S
Leticia's
Little Henry's
Little Italy
Little Joe's
London Wine Bar, The
Long Life Vegi House
Lori's Diner
Los Chiles
MacArthur Park
Mai's
Mandalay
Mandarin House
Manora's Thai Cuisine
Marin Joe's
Max's Diner
Max's Opera Cafe
Mekong
Mel's Diner
Mifune

Mikado
Mike's Chinese Cuisine
Milano Joe's
Milano Pizzeria
Milly's
Miz Brown's Feed Bag
Moishe's Pipick
Mustard's Grill/N
Nan Yang
Narai
Narsai's Cafe
New Joe's
Nicaragua Restaurant
North Beach Restaurant
North India Rest.
Ocean City
Ocean Restaurant
Original Joe's
Original Old Clam Hse.
Osome
Panama Hotel
Paolo's/S
Pasha
Pasta Moon
Peacock, The
Perry's
Phnom Penh
Pier 23 Cafe
Plearn Thai Cuisine
Riera's
Rio Grill/S
Ristorante Fabrizio
Ronayne's
Roosevelt Tamale
Rotunda, The
Ruby's
S. Asimakopoulous
Sally's
San Francisco BBQ
Sanppo
Saul's Delicatessen
Savannah Grill
Schroeder's
Scott's Seafood Grill/S
Seoul Garden
Shelly's Italian
Siam Cuisine
South China Cafe
Spenger's Fish Grotto
Spuntino
Squid's Cafe
Straits Cafe
Swan Oyster Depot
Taco Al Pastor/S
Taiwan Restaurant
Tanuki
Taqueria Mission
Thep Phanom

Ti Bacio
Tien Fu
Tommaso's
Tommy's Joynt
Ton Kiang
Tortola Restaurant
Trader Vic's
Trattoria Contadina
Trio Cafe
Triple Rock Brewery
Tu Lan
Tung Fong
Uncle Yu's
U.S. Restaurant
Vegi Food
Via Veneto
Vicolo Pizzeria
Victorian Garden Rest./S
Vines/N
Vivande Porta Via
Washington Sq. Bar/Grill
Waterfront Restaurant
Yamato Sukiyaki Hse.
Yet Wah
Yoshida-Ya
Yoshi's Rest.
Yuen Yung
Yuet Lee
Yujean's
Zola's

Benihana
Bill's Place
Blue Light Cafe
Bohemian Cigar Store
Cadillac Bar & Rest.
Caribbean Zone
Chevys
Clark's by the Bay/S
Ernesto's
Fat Apple's
Flynn's Landing
Green's
Guaymas
Hamburger Mary's
Hard Rock Cafe
Julie's Supper Club
Little City Antipasti Bar
MacArthur Park
Max's Diner
Max's Opera Cafe
Mel's Diner
New Joe's
Perry's
690
Southside*
Splendido's
Spuntino
Stars Cafe
Straits Cafe
Tommaso's
Tommy's Joynt
Triple Rock Brewery
Vicolo Pizzeria
(*Not in *Survey*)

Teas
(Check times and prices)

Acropolis Deli
Barnaby's By The Bay/N
Campton Place Hotel*
Celadon
Cheer's Cafe
Donatello Hotel*
Fournou's Oven
French Room, The
Lafayette on Pacific
L'Entrecote de Paris
Little City Antipasti Bar
Mark Hopkins Hotel*
Rotunda, The
Silks
Spuntino
Vines/N
(*Not in *Survey*)

Teenagers and Other Youthful Spirits

Ace Cafe
Balboa Cafe
Basta Pasta

Valet Parking

Alfred's
Alta Mira Restaurant
Asta
Basta Pasta
Bella Voce
Bentley's
Big Four
Blue Fox, The
Cafe Majestic
California Cafe Bar & Grill
Calif. Culinary Academy
Campton Place
Caprice, The
Casa Madrona
Donatello
Ernie's
Etrusca
Fleur de Lys
Fior d'Italia
Fog City Diner
Fournou's Oven

French Room, The
Hard Rock Cafe
Harris' Restaurant
Horizons
House of Prime Rib
Jack's
Janot's
John Ash & Co./N
Julius' Castle
Korea House
Le Castel
Le Club
L'Entrecote de Paris
Les Saisons/S
Le St. Tropez
Maltese Grill
Mandarin, The
Masa's
Maye's Oyster House
Mela
New San Remo
North Beach Restaurant
1001 Nob Hill Rest.
Pacific Grill
Pacific Hts. Bar/Grill
Park Grill
Pasha
Peacock, The
Pierre at Meridien
Postrio
Prego Ristorante
Regina's
Ristorante Grifone
Rodin
Rosalie's
Sardine Factory/S
Scoma's
Scott's Seafood Grill/S
Shadows, The
Square One
Squire Restaurant
Stanford Park
Trader Vic's
Tutto Bene
Victor's
Washington Sq. Bar/Grill
Waterfront Restaurant
Wu Kong
Yoshi's Rest.

Visitors on Expense Accounts

Amelio's
Auberge du Soleil/N
Big Four
Blue Fox, The

Campton Place
Carnelian Room
Chez Panisse
Chez T.J./S
Domaine Chandon/N
Donatello
Ernie's
Fleur de Lys
Fournou's Oven
French Room, The
Harris' Restaurant
John Ash & Co./N
Le Castel
Le Club
Les Saisons/S
Masa's
Nob Hill Restaurant
Park Grill
Pierre at Meridien
Postrio
Square One
Squire Restaurant
Stars
Trader Vic's

Winning Wine Lists

Ace Cafe
Acqurello
Adriatic Restaurant
Amelio's
A. Sabella's
Auberge du Soleil/N*
Barbarossa/S
Bay Wolf
Bella Vista
Big Four
Bix
Blue Fox, The*
Blue Light Cafe
Brasserie Tomo
Buca Giovani
Bucci's
Cafe at Chez Panisse
Calif. Culinary Academy
Campton Place*
Caprice, The
Carnelian Room*
Celadon
Chateau Souverain/N
Chez Panisse*
Chez T.J./S
Christophe
Dal Baffo
Domaine Chandon/N*
Donatello
Doug's BBQ

El Paseo
Emile's/S
Empress of China
Enoteca Lanzone
Ernie's*
Etrusca
Flea Street Cafe
Fleur de Lys*
Fournou's Oven*
Fourth Street Grill
French Laundry/N
French Room, The*
Fresh Cream/S
Green's
Grille, The
Harris' Restaurant
Imperial Palace
Jack's
Janot's
Jin Jiang Kee Joon
John Ash & Co./N*
Julius' Castle
Lafayette on Pacific
La Folie
La Foret/S
Lalime's
Lark Creek Inn*
Lascaux
Le Central
Le Club
Le Metropole
Le Mouton Noir/S
L'Entrecote de Paris
Le Papillon/S
Le Piano Zinc
L'Escargot
Les Saisons/S
Le St. Tropez
L'Horizon Restaurant/S
London Wine Bar, The
Madrona Manor/N
Mandarin, The
Masa's*
Mustard's Grill/N
Nob Hill Restaurant*
North India Rest.
Old Swiss House
1001 Nob Hill Rest.
Pacific Grill
Pacific Hts. Bar/Grill*
Paolo's/S
Park Grill
Pasta Moon
Pavilion Room
Piatti/N
Pierre at Meridien
Plearn Thai Cuisine
Plumed Horse, The/S

Postrio
Premier Cru Cafe
Rio Grill/S
Ristorante Fabrizio
Santa Fe Bar/Grill
Shadows, The
Silks
Square One*
Squire Restaurant*
Starmont/N*
Stars*
Tourelle
Trader Vic's*
Tra Vigne/N
231 Ellsworth
Umberto's
Vanessi's
Victor's*
Yujean's
Zuni Cafe
(*Truly outstanding)

Worth a Trip

NORTH
Geyserville
  Chateau Souverain
Mendocino
  Cafe Beaujolais
Pt. Reyes
  Station House Cafe
Rutherford
  Auberge du Soleil
Santa Rosa
  John Ash & Co.
Sonoma
  Grille, The
St. Helena
  Starmont
  Terra
  Tra Vigne
Yountville
  Domaine Chandon
  French Laundry
  Mustard's Grill
  Piatti
SOUTH
Monterey
  Fresh Cream
  Sardine Factory
  Central
Mountain View
  Chez T.J.
San Jose
  Emile's
  Le Papillon
Saratoga
  Le Mouton Noir

Young Children
(Besides fast-food places)

Abalonetti
Alejandro's Sociedad
Basta Pasta
Benihana
Bill's Place
Brother's Delicatessen
Cafe Riggio
China Station
Chu Lin
Cliff House
Empress of China
Ernesto's
Fat Apple's
Hahn's Hibachi
Hard Rock Cafe
Kan's
King of China
Kirin
La Taqueria
Little Italy
Little Joe's
Marin Joe's
Max's Diner
Mel's Diner
Mifune
Milano Pizzeria
Miz Brown's Feed Bag
Original Joe's
Sam's Anchor Cafe
Samurai
San Francisco BBQ
Scott's Seafood Grill/S
Sears Fine Foods
Seoul Garden
Spenger's Fish Grotto
Station House Cafe/N
Swan Oyster Depot
Tommaso's
Ton Kiang
Trader Vic's
Vicolo Pizzeria
Yet Wah

NOTES

WINE VINTAGE CHART 1979-1989

These ratings are designed to help you select wine to go with your meal. They are on the same 0 to 30 scale used throughout this Guide. The ratings reflect both the quality of the vintage year and the wine's readiness to drink. Thus, if a wine is not fully mature or is over the hill, its rating has been reduced. The ratings were prepared principally by our friend, Howard Strawitz, a law professor at the University of South Carolina.

WHITES	79	80	81	82	83	84	85	86	87	88	89
French:											
Burgundy	17	—	16	18	19	14	25	28	16	21	24
Loire Valley	—	—	—	—	—	—	19	18	15	20	23
Champagne	20	—	19	23	20	—	21	19	—	—	22
Sauternes	12	24	23	13	23	—	18	23	10	25	24
California:											
Chardonnay	—	16	14	13	13	22	24	27	24	26	24
REDS											
French:											
Bordeaux	22	13	25	27	24	15	25	24	21	21	21
Burgundy	18	20	16	20	25	14	27	16	21	20	19
Rhone	18	17	16	16	25	15	25	21	16	19	20
Beaujolais	—	—	—	—	—	—	21	22	23	24	26
California: Cabernet Sauvignon	20	23	21	23	18	26	25	23	24	18	19
Zinfandel	—	—	—	—	—	17	18	16	20	15	16
Italian:*											
Chianti	11	—	14	17	13	—	23	16	12	20	11
Piedmont	21	12	15	25	14	—	23	13	17	19	20

* Bargain sippers take note—Certain wines are reliable year in year out and are reasonably priced as well. These wines are best in the most recent vintages. They include: Alsacian Pinot Blancs, Cotes de Rhone, Muscadet, Bardolino, Valpolicella, Corvo, Spanish Rioja and California Zinfandel.